Tony Carter

The Aftermath of Reengineering
Downsizing and Corporate Performance

The Aftermath
of Reengineering
Downsizing and Corporate Performance

HAWORTH Marketing Resources
Innovations in Practice & Professional Services
William J. Winston, Senior Editor

New, Recent, and Forthcoming Titles:

Internal Marketing: Your Company's Next Stage of Growth by Dennis J. Cahill

The Clinician's Guide to Managed Behavioral Care by Norman Winegar

Marketing Health Care into the Twenty-First Century: The Changing Dynamic by Alan K. Vitberg

Fundamentals of Strategic Planning for Health-Care Organizations edited by Stan Williamson, Robert Stevens, David Loudon, and R. Henry Migliore

Risky Business: Managing Violence in the Workplace by Lynne Falkin McClure

Predicting Successful Hospital Mergers and Acquisitions: A Financial and Marketing Analytical Tool by David P. Angrisani and Robert L. Goldman

Marketing Research That Pays Off: Case Histories of Marketing Research Leading to Success in the Marketplace edited by Larry Percy

How Consumers Pick a Hotel: Strategic Segmentation and Target Marketing by Dennis Cahill

Applying Telecommunications and Technology from a Global Business Perspective by Jay Zajas and Olive Church

Strategic Planning for Private Higher Education by Carle M. Hunt, Kenneth W. Oosting, Robert Stevens, David Loudon, and R. Henry Migliore

Writing for Money in Mental Health by Douglas H. Ruben

The New Business Values for Success in the Twenty-First Century: Improvement, Innovation, Inclusion, Incentives, Information by John Persico and Patricia Rouner Morris

Marketing Planning Guide, Second Edition by Robert E. Stevens, David L. Loudon, Bruce Wrenn, and William E. Warren

Contemporary Sales Force Management by Tony Carter

4 × 4 Leadership and the Purpose of the Firm by H. H. Pete Bradshaw

Lessons in Leisure Business Success: The Recreation Professional's Business Transformation Primer by Jonathan T. Scott

Guidebook to Managed Care and Practice Management Terminology by Norman Winegar and Michelle L. Hayter

Medical Group Management in Turbulent Times: How Physician Leadership Can Optimize Health Plan, Hospital, and Medical Group Performance by Paul A. Sommers

Defining Your Market: Winning Strategies for High-Tech, Industrial, and Service Firms by Art Weinstein

Alignment: A Provider's Guide to Managing the Practice of Health Care by Paul A. Sommers

Consumer Satisfaction in Medical Practice by Paul A. Sommers

Using Public Relations Strategies to Promote Your Nonprofit Organization by Ruth Ellen Kinzey

The Aftermath of Reengineering: Downsizing and Corporate Performance by Tony Carter

Principles of Advertising: A Global Perspective by Monle Lee and Carla Johnson

The Aftermath
of Reengineering
Downsizing and Corporate Performance

Tony Carter

The Haworth Press
New York • London • Oxford

The Haworth Press, Inc., 10 Alice Street, Binghamton, NY 13904-1580

Cover design by Marylouise E. Doyle.

Library of Congress Cataloging-in-Publication Data

Carter, Tony, 1955-
    The aftermath of reengineering : downsizing and corporate performance / Tony Carter.
        p.   cm.
    Includes bibliographical references and index.
    ISBN 0-7890-0720-7 (alk. paper)
    1. Reengineering (Management). 2. Downsizing of organizations. I. Title.
HD58.87.C37 1999
658.4'063—dc21
                                                  99-16947
                                                      CIP

ABOUT THE AUTHOR

Tony Carter, JD, MBA, is Associate Professor and Chair of the Business Administration and Professional programs at Wagner College in Staten Island, New York, where he is also on the faculty of the Executive MBA Program. In addition, he is Adjunct Professor of Marketing at the Graduate School of Business of Columbia University where he teaches in the MBA program and has taught in the Executive MBA Program. At Columbia University, Dr. Carter is also the Associate Faculty Director of the Executive Management Program for sales managers. The author of the book *Contemporary Sales Force Management* (The Haworth Press, Inc.), Dr. Carter has written articles that have been published in the *Harvard Business Review,* the *Columbia Journal of World Business, Business Week,* the *Journal of Professional Services Marketing,* the *Journal of Global Competitiveness, Sales and Marketing Management, Management Magazine, Selling Power,* the *Journal of Economic Literature,* the *Journal of Personal Selling and Sales Management,* and the *Journal of Employment.*

Dr. Carter has worked as a manager for several corporations. His case studies and research on marketing, sales, and management have been adopted and used by various universities and organizations around the world. Dr. Carter has conducted research in the European Union in Belgium, The People's Republic of China, and Poland. Still an active consultant, he works on management, sales, and marketing issues for a variety of companies worldwide. Dr. Carter is the recipient of *The Wall Street Journal* Award and is an Inductee of Delta Mu Delta, The National Honor Society in Business Administration.

To Mary, Walter, and Calvin,
my parents,
Walter Palin, Mike, and his family,
Jerzy, Maria, and their family

CONTENTS

Foreword   xi
Ambassador Ulric Haynes, Jr.

Preface   xiii

SECTION I: INTRODUCTION

Chapter 1. Management and Reengineering   3

Introduction   3
Reengineering's Dark Side: Layoffs   4
The Essence of Reengineering   12
Management's Role   14
Efficient Organizations   14
Strategic and Societal Consequences   15
Case Study   18

Chapter 2. Reengineering's Consequences   21

Introduction   21
The Human Side of Reengineering   22
New Rules in the Business Environment   27
Case Study   32

SECTION II: PRACTICAL OUTCOMES

Chapter 3. Urgency Theory   37

Introduction   37
Effective Reengineering   39
Applying Urgency Theory   40
Employee Performance   51
Case Study   52

Chapter 4. Customer Focus   55

Introduction   55
Customers and Reengineering   56
Case Study   65

Chapter 5. New Management Tools   **67**

Introduction   67
Business Process Reengineering   67
Business Reengineering   68
Balanced Scorecard   70
Virtual Offices   74
Outsourcing   77
Technology   78
Modularity   82
Crisis/Risk Management   83
Boards and Council Concept   88
Business Agility   89
Case Study   89

SECTION III: STRATEGIC DEVELOPMENTS

Chapter 6. Organizational Communication   **95**

Introduction   95
Reengineering Goals   96
Business Communication   99
Effective Communication   101
Business Meetings   103
Business Research   103
Empowerment   104
Teams   106
Case Study   111

Chapter 7. Professional Development and Learning   **115**

Introduction   115
Effective Practices of Companies That Achieve
    Competitive Success   116
Performance Measurement Systems   119
Measurement   120
Learning Organization   123
Part-Time Employment   126
Case Study   127

SECTION IV: EXAMINATION OF VARIOUS ORGANIZATIONS AND REENGINEERING

Chapter 8. An Evaluation of Best Practices Resulting from Reengineering   **133**

Introduction   133
AT&T   133
Restructuring the IBM Sales Force   135
Hewlett-Packard and Reengineering   138
Health Care and Reengineering   140
Pennsylvania State Employees Credit Union   143
Personal Restructuring   143
Integration Management   145
Conclusion   146
Case Study   147

Notes   **149**

Index   **159**

Foreword

As a long-time admirer of Tony Carter, I am all the more proud of the challenge he throws out to the business world to use reengineering as a means to drive managerial improvement. In so doing, he correctly and forcefully argues against using it to justify predetermined decisions or, worse yet, as the rationale behind short-term cost-cutting actions.

In this book, Carter correctly focuses on those managerial techniques that drive reengineering without excluding consideration of those business practices that are impacted. In this connection, using a case study to conclude each chapter makes the book a most useful guide for business practitioners, business scholars, and students of business alike.

At the same time, the author does not shrink from emphasizing implicitly that an all-important goal of reengineering is to simultaneously link serving the needs of the customer (the market), of the employees (the producers), and of the owner/shareholders (the profit-seekers). Since each one of us falls into one or more of these categories, there are important messages contained in this book for us all.

Ambassador Ulric Haynes, Jr.
Former Dean, Frank G. Zarb School of Business
Hofstra University
Israel

Preface

Throughout my work on this book, the old adage that "change is the only constant in life" was always on my mind. Let's face it, as sophisticated as reengineering is, change is the real underlying premise of this management tool. Reengineering is based on the concept of significantly altering existing models and thinking and using dramatic improvements that are accomplished by reinventing the way in which work is done. It is characterized as the radical redesign of an organization's business processes to achieve strategic breakthroughs. Volatile business conditions have driven the use of reengineering and have led to drastic corporate downsizing so that organizations are expected to do more with less. However, has reengineering accomplished its objectives of breakthrough results for organizations and achieving huge advances in sales performance levels?

Reengineering, as a management tool, should be aimed at creating efficient, more focused organizations with reinvigorated sales activity. Has "the aftermath of reengineering" instead resulted in additional people management and resource management burdens for managers and employees that deny them the opportunity to maximize their performance capability?

The Aftermath of Reengineering is organized into four sections. Section I, the introduction, includes Chapter 1, "Management and Reengineering," and Chapter 2, "Reengineering's Consequences." Section II focuses on practical outcomes and includes Chapter 3, "Urgency Theory," Chapter 4, "Customer Focus," and Chapter 5, "New Management Tools." Section III covers strategic development in Chapter 6, "Organizational Communication," and Chapter 7, "Professional Development and Learning." Section IV evaluates various organizations and reengineering efforts in Chapter 8, "An Evaluation of Best Practices Resulting from Reengineering." Each chapter ends with a fairly brief, complex, and, in some instances, abstract case study, similar to what managers face, that warrants an application of the chapter's subject matter.

I conducted my research through the existing literature and through the use of a survey of ninety-two organizations, many of them Fortune 500 corporations, that have used reengineering. The book explores whether most organizations are significantly effective following their reengineering efforts. Hopefully, business students at the undergraduate, MBA, and executive education levels, managers, salespeople, entrepreneurs, and consultants will find this book unique and extremely useful.

Special thanks to Bill Winston and the rest of the editorial staff at The Haworth Press for the confidence and support they gave me while I wrote this book. I am especially grateful to Ambassador Ulric Haynes for his encouragement and the inspiration that he has given me and many others through his own extraordinary professional accomplishments. Over the years, I have truly been honored to consider him a mentor and a friend. Last, I extend my sincere appreciation to "my close friends" Walter Rohrs of Wagner College and Noel Capon of Columbia University's Graduate School of Business. They constantly challenge themselves and those around them to improve and to attain the next level. They are both the true inspiration for this book.

Tony Carter
Staten Island, New York

SECTION I:
INTRODUCTION

Chapter 1

Management and Reengineering

INTRODUCTION

Volatile business conditions have led to drastic corporate downsizing, meaning organizations are expected to do more with less. Managers must also be more knowledgeable and possess a more eclectic myriad of business skills, many of which have not even been seen until recently. Many internal and external changes have occurred to organizations that have dictated the need to do business differently. Changes such as technological advances, globalization, catastrophic business crises, a more frantic competitive climate, and more demanding, sophisticated customers are examples of some of the shifts in the external business environment. Internal changes to organizations have been in the form of reengineering, accompanied by structural realignments and downsizing, greater emphasis on quality levels in product and service output, faster communication channels, and a more educated, skilled employee base with higher expectations from management. (See Table 1.1 for issues to consider during the reengineering process.)

By using reengineering, managers can ensure that the organization is ready for any changes that may occur. If used as a one-dimensional, quick-fix solution, reengineering will just lead to downsizing and poor strategic business results. More than 3.4 million jobs have been cut by Fortune 500 companies. The results of reengineering efforts have caused increased costs and decreased productivity. The obsession to look good at any price has cost organizations their most valuable resource—capable people. Reengineering that results in staff cuts to save money is not always in the best interest of the organization. The survivors may also feel loss, betrayal, distrust, become less productive, and avoid risk-taking situations. Middle managers alone have been the primary targets for over 20 percent of downsizing efforts.[1]

TABLE 1.1. Significant Issues for Reengineering

• Core Competencies	• Identifying Lucrative Markets
• Competitive Advantage	• Necessary Expenses
• Anticipating Changes in Future Markets	• Effective Time Management
	• Employee Empowerment
• Understanding How Customers Define Value	• Establishing Critical Processes
• Setting Profit Growth Targets	• Developing Relevant Processes for Customers

REENGINEERING'S DARK SIDE: LAYOFFS

Chase

Chase Manhattan Corporation, attempting to cut down a bloated bureaucracy and steep overhead expenses, is in the midst of a corporate restructuring that could involve laying off as much as one-third of its 9,400-strong administrative staff. The layoffs would mark the biggest round of staff cuts at Chase since Chemical Banking Corporation acquired the bank in 1996. At the time, the new Chase announced its intent to eliminate as many as 12,000 of the combined banks' roughly 73,000 positions. Though Chase carried out most of those cuts through layoffs and attrition, additional hiring in other areas offset many of the reductions. Currently, Chase's staff numbers 69,000, up about 1,200 from a year ago. People inside the company say they expect the layoffs to involve about 3,000 employees. These dismissals have hurt morale among some administrative workers awaiting word on their future. Most of the expected staff cuts would affect middle-level and low-level employees in the marketing, corporate communications, personnel, legal, and finance departments. It remains unclear how much money Chase will save through the restructuring. Analysts predict the figure will more likely be in the tens of millions of dollars rather than in the hundreds of millions.[2]

Eastman Kodak

Eastman Kodak Company announced that it was planning to chop 10,000 employees from its payroll as part of a broad plan to trim $1 billion from its annual costs. One reason for the steep decline in Kodak's stock after the restructuring announcement is skepticism by analysts about whether Kodak's cost cutting went deep enough. If Kodak is not laying off some 10,000 employees, it may not be able to boost productivity or profit as much as investors expected. Kodak is also making analysis of its restructuring announcement difficult by not saying what its current level of employment is. The company reported earlier that it had 94,800 employees at the end of 1996, but has not since updated that figure. Some analysts wonder if Kodak managers are using round numbers such as 10,000 jobs and $1 billion in cost reductions to boost investors' confidence. Standard & Poor's Rating Agency placed $489 million of Kodak debt on Credit Watch because of concerns about the gradual pace of cost reductions and the need to quickly boost productivity to offset pricing and currency pressures. It noted that Kodak's debt has risen to almost $1 billion from $200 million a year ago as a result of acquisitions and share repurchases that have exceeded free cash flow. Kodak's senior debt currently has a double-A-minus rating.[3]

IBM

International Business Machines Corporation has begun sending layoff notices to hundreds of employees in its North American division as part of a major restructuring of the unit's sales and distribution organization. The news came in a memo to employees from John W. Thompson, general manager of the White Plains, New York, division, which has about 20,000 employees, mostly in sales and distribution. In the memo, Thompson said that given previous job cuts in his operation, a voluntary job-reduction program "doesn't make sense." The restructuring will consolidate sales and distribution between product and customer groups, eliminating the current geographic structure. Thompson said the division was being revamped because customers have complained that the current structure is "too slow and difficult to do business with." Moreover, he said, "as more of our revenue comes from lower-margin offerings, we cannot afford all the structure we have in place today. In the past, IBM often reacted too slowly to changes in the marketplace. Now we are determined to be ahead of the curve." IBM, Armonk, New York, has about 240,000 employees worldwide, including 119,000 in the United States alone. The company has said the overall cutback program is needed to reduce costs as it has had trouble increasing revenue rapidly.[4]

IBM is also exploring new partnerships to achieve breakthrough results. Although IBM is the world's largest maker of computers, their personal computer business has been struggling for several years due to sluggish sales and price wars that have squeezed profits. Recently, IBM and Dell, two of the computer industry's biggest rivals, entered a deal in which Dell agreed to buy $16 billion of IBM equipment over the next seven years. The two companies also agreed to jointly develop new technology and give each other previews of future products. For IBM, the deal helps ensure a steady and increasing flow of business from a company that is already one of its largest customers.[5]

J. P. Morgan

Dwindling business in Asian equities has forced J. P. Morgan & Company to trim 100 people from its 1,700 staff in the region. The Asian staff reduction forms part of the U.S.-based investment bank's drive to tighten its cost base. Its head office in New York announced that the bank planned to cut 5 percent, or 700 staff, from its global head count of 14,000. Other cuts are being made in Singapore, Sydney, and Tokyo, targeting areas where customer demand has been declining. In Asia, volatile market conditions have dulled the investment appetite of international fund managers.

With the retrenchment, J. P. Morgan plans to focus on investment banking-related activities, including its investment banking advisory operations, cross-border financing, private equity transactions, direct investment, and the structuring of innovative financings.[6]

Digital Equipment

Compaq Computer Corporation plans to cut about 15,000 jobs at Digital Equipment Corporation, or about 28 percent of the company's workforce, after Compaq's proposed acquisition of Digital is completed, according to people familiar with the matter. The layoffs will most likely come from Digital's personal computer division, some parts of its sales force, and some corporate computer operations that overlap with Compaq's business. Digital had about 53,500 employees, and at its peak in the late 1980s, Digital's workforce topped 130,000. Compaq has about 31,500 employees.

Digital's Chairman and Chief Executive Robert B. Palmer was eligible for an adjusted 1998 bonus for leaving Digital before the end of June. After the deal is completed, Palmer will be eligible to acquire just over $1 million in stock options. Digital's average cost of all the options is about $45, which would give them a value of about $14 million.[7]

Compaq is looking to expand its sales among corporate customers, and the services business was one of the main reasons the world's personal computer leader agreed to purchase Digital.[8] Unfortunately, absent a crisis, few companies spend time thinking about how to retain corporate vitality. The computer industry was once the most farsighted and revolutionary in America. Although no company can be the sole source of innovation, simply buying up someone else's creativity is a poor substitute. In a competitive environment, innovation is everything; as DEC learned, having good growth strategy is not enough. A company that wants to remain ahead has to institutionalize constant innovation, just as companies once learned how to make quality a part of every aspect of their operations.

Chrysler

Chrysler Corporation, the No. 3 automaker, has allied with Germany's Daimler-Benz Ag. It is important for the survival of Chrysler to diversify themselves and expand to become a more global company. It is up to the financial management of the corporation to make these kinds of decisions.[9]

Bankers Trust

Bankers Trust New York Corporation is adjusting to the slower business climate in Asia by exploring a restructuring of its Asia-Pacific operations that could lead to layoffs. Bankers Trust's restructuring would make it the latest foreign bank to scale back in the wake of Asia's financial crisis. They have 1,500 employees in the region, excluding Australia and New Zealand. The bank has offices in twelve Asian countries.[10]

Airbus

Airbus is not just redesigning the way it makes parts, it is redesigning itself and the way it works. To pull out of an early 1990s slump, Airbus streamlined production and slashed jobs, enabling it to speed up deliveries while cutting prices. Now, it is capturing a growing slice of the business. Last year, its firm orders rose 50 percent to a record 460 jets valued at $29.6 billion, giving it a 45 percent market share—an astonishing achievement, given that early in the 1990s, its share hovered around 30 percent.

The changes have enabled Airbus to slash its lead time—the period from when a customer gives its specifications until delivery—to nine months from fifteen for its single-aisle planes and to twelve months from eighteen for wide-bodies. As a result, cash-consuming inventories are reduced 30 percent.[11]

Data General

Data General Corporation, struggling to return to profitability, expects to cut about 400 jobs worldwide, about 8 percent of its total workforce, and will discontinue development of an inexpensive line of Internet computer servers for which it once had high hopes. Data General said it would boost its computer storage business by adding jobs and increasing sales and research support. The company's storage business, which accounts for about one-third of its revenue, has come under competitive pressure.[12]

KLM

KLM Royal Dutch Airlines is one of the cornerstones of Alitalia's race to reverse years of inefficiencies to survive in a consolidating and increasingly competitive market. As for the link with KLM, Alitalia and the Dutch carrier will integrate their flight networks, redistributing routes to take advantage of the multihub systems the alliance creates.[13]

Motorola

Motorola, Incorporated, provided one of the first indications of the damage done to American multinationals by the declining Asian markets: fourth-quarter earnings were moderately below analysts' expectations, as cellular phone sales in Asia fell and major orders for cell phone systems dropped significantly.[14] Motorola disclosed radical steps to stanch its steadily eroding profits and market share, announcing a layoff of 10 percent of its workforce, or 15,000 workers, and a $1.95 billion charge to pay for the mass firings and a consolidation of its semiconductor and paging operations.

The company, once the leader of the burgeoning wireless communications industry, has suffered in the past three years. Global demand has shifted from the analog cellular phones and networks Motorola dominated to a digital era requiring more expertise in software, computing, and end-to-end network reliability. In addition, demand for its consumer products in Asia imploded during the past year with the currency crises there, while price wars and glut became endemic in some of its cell phone and pager markets.

The company's decline stands in sharp contrast to the general ascendance of American high-tech companies worldwide in recent years. Yet other technology giants are increasingly troubled by chronic price wars and slowing demand. However, those big companies are still highly profitable. Motorola's biggest direct competitors—including Lucent Technologies, Incorporated, Telefon L. M. Ericcson, and Northern Telecom Limited—are prospering in the age of digital communications networks. In that context, the prospect of an operating loss, Motorola's first since the flat mid-1980s, is shocking. Moreover, on a percentage basis, the layoffs are Motorola's largest since the mid-1970s.[15]

Nabisco

Facing sluggish cookie and cracker sales, Nabisco Holdings Corporation cut 3,500 jobs, or 6 percent of its workforce. The broad retrenchment is part of Nabisco's rehabilitation plan, engineered by James M. Kilts, who arrived as president and chief executive officer of the maker of Oreos, Chips Ahoy!, Nutter Butter cookies, and Ritz crackers. Kilts also plans to boost marketing spending by 30 percent on its core cookie and cracker brands in the second half of this year.

Nabisco recently has posted disappointing profits amid rising competition in its core biscuit business. So Nabisco, similar to other big food companies lately, is stepping up basic marketing—from TV commercials to Sunday coupon inserts—to increase brand sales. Competitors such as Campbell Soup Company, Vlasic Foods International, and H. J. Heinz Company have also boosted marketing spending to increase sales. Thinning ad budgets, especially, can make national food brands vulnerable to cheaper rivals, particularly store brands.[16]

Xerox

Xerox Corporation plans to eliminate about 9,000 jobs over two years as the company attempts to control costs that remain higher than those of its new competitors. The job cuts, which affect about 10 percent of Xerox's 91,400 worldwide employees, come as the copier maker is enjoying record earnings, a surging stock price, and a renewed focus. However, Xerox is at a turning point: it needs to spend heavily to roll out new, less expensive digital copiers as it finds ways to trim a high-cost structure designed mostly for its still-lucrative traditional copiers.

Xerox expects to save as much as $1 billion annually once all the changes are in place. The Stamford, Connecticut, company has 150 revamping projects under way, including consolidating country-specific operations in Europe into a single entity, reducing parts depots in the United States, and outsourcing storage and distribution functions.[17]

Sunbeam

Sunbeam Corporation has plans to eliminate 5,100 jobs. The Delray Beach, Florida, maker of appliances and camping equipment is in a time of transition. The job cuts will result from closing two plants in Mexico, one in Costa Rica, and five in the United States, as well as from cutbacks at their newly acquired companies and a greater reliance on outsourcing. Sunbeam will sell three Coleman units: the East Pak Backpack division and units making electric generators and hot tubs. The company expects those sales to yield pretax proceeds totaling about $250 million to $350 million.[18]

GTE

GTE Corporation announced a major program to cut costs and raise cash to increase its financial flexibility and grow more competitive. The Stamford, Connecticut-based, local and long distance company announced actions to undertake a merger or other transaction at a time of intense merger activity in the telecommunications business. GTE has been rumored to be a possible candidate to combine with British Telecommunications PLC or to acquire Qwest Communication International, Incorporated, which is putting together a high-capacity fiber-optics communications network.[19]

General Mills

General Mills today is a trimmer, more focused food maker, with new top management, a reorganized sales force, and manufacturing plants. A twenty-one-year veteran of General Mills with a background in marketing, Mark Sanger took over when longtime chairman and CEO H. Brewster Atwater Jr. retired.

"We don't want to be the world's biggest food company, but we do want to be the world's most innovative food company," Sanger says. "Food categories are absolutely driven by new products, product improvements, and marketing innovations." Consumers experienced a flurry of "new" and "improved" products as the company sought to reverse share losses in key categories.[20] Breakfast cereals clearly are General Mills' most important product, providing 40 percent of $5.03 billion in sales, despite an 8 percent volume decline. To reinvigorate its cereal sales, the company has made sugar-frosted versions of two old reliables, Cheerios and Wheaties. Sales to retailers during the first eight days totaled a robust $25 million.

Overseas, where General Mills was a latecomer, Sanger is pushing for rapid growth. Recently, international sales accounted for 14 percent of total sales. But, if the company exports more fruit snacks, that proportion could be 25 percent by the year 2000. General Mills already sells cereals and salty snacks through joint ventures and will launch a third venture, desserts, in Latin America.

THE ESSENCE OF REENGINEERING

Reengineering is based on the concept of significantly altering existing models and thinking. It means using dramatic improvements that are accomplished by reinventing the way in which work is done. It is this method of radical improvement that makes reengineering so different and so compelling. Since reengineering finds better ways to give customers what they want, while achieving huge advances in performance, it provides a competitive advantage that impacts the bottom line.

There is a human side to reengineering that helps drive the entire effort. These human elements can involve a vision for the future, new workplace values, involved leadership, teamwork, and customer-driven processes. The changes brought about through reengineering require new skills for people organizations.

A definition of business process reengineering is "the radical redesign of an organization's operations and management to achieve strategic breakthroughs." Reengineering means starting over at the beginning. It means taking apart the way work is done, thinking "outside the box," and then re-creating it in a totally new format. This is an effort that has long-term effects.

So if a reengineering effort is so demanding, what motivates an organization to use this process? Customers are a lot more knowledgeable and demanding than ever before. They know what they want, and there are a lot of competitors around who can and will get it for them faster, cheaper, and designed specifically for their needs. Reengineering can re-create the organization so that it can be competitive, flexible, and able to move with greater speed. Reengineering can mean survival.

Business process reengineering projects have shown that some techniques and methodologies to achieving success involve the use of teams, benchmarking, organizational rationalization, business reviews, data/workflow analysis, redesign, and capacity planning. These are effective tools that can yield positive change.

Reengineering, also known as process innovation and core process redesign, is the search for, and implementation of, radical change in business processes to achieve breakthrough results. Its chief tool is a clean sheet of paper. Most change efforts start with what exists and fix it up. Reengineering, adherents emphasize, is not tweaking old procedures, and certainly not plain-vanilla downsizing, nor is it a program for bottom-up continuous improvement. Reengineers start from the future and work backward, as if unconstrained by existing methods, people, or departments (see Figures 1.1 and 1.2).

FIGURE 1.1. Percentage of Managers Who Expected Further Reengineering to Take Place in Their Firms

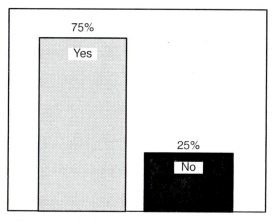

Source: Carter Reengineering Survey (1998).

FIGURE 1.2. Percentage of Organizations That Have Gone Through Reengineering Between 1993 and 1998

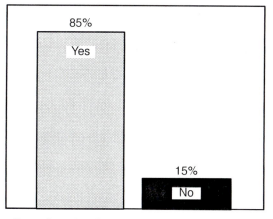

Source: Carter Reengineering Survey (1998).

MANAGEMENT'S ROLE

Years of relentless downsizing, "right-sizing," and reengineering in corporate America are all aimed in part at shedding excess bureaucracy. It is certainly true that tens of thousands of middle managers have lost their jobs in recent years, and many face long, painful struggles in trying to replace them. It also is true that even for many managers who stay employed, the flattening of hierarchies cuts promotion opportunities.

Yet other economic forces are offsetting these losses and creating management work where it did not exist before. The "de-layering" seen in the great reengineering of corporate hierarchies spreads out management work and endows some rank-and-file employees with managerial responsibilities. Technologies that supplant workers require managers to oversee them, as does outsourcing. The growing complexity of white-collar work increases the need for management in some cases. A shift in management duties toward external dealings with customers, rather than just supervision of employees, blurs the distinction between managers and marketers.

The reality of reengineering is that many more people are in a decision-making mode, so more people get elevated to a management category. Often changes in the marketplace create new managerial requirements. As the health care business shifts toward managed care, American Home Products Corporation has restructured its sales and marketing. Although the sales force has been cut by 30 percent, managers overseeing medical center accounts have increased fourfold, in part because such accounts require closer attention.

EFFICIENT ORGANIZATIONS

In the business world, fat is out and flat is in. The reason is that hierarchy breeds bureaucracy and removing it allows people to make their own decisions. This type of empowerment, in turn, improves efficiency. Many employees are becoming disillusioned by the disappearance of prospects for promotion and other traditional goals in their de-layered workplace. Flatter structures destroy any illusions about career prospects that many employees are able to maintain in a more hierarchical structure.[21]

In 1985, 406,000 people worked for IBM, which made profits of $6.6 billion. One-third of the people, and all of the profits, are now gone. Automaker Volkswagen says it needs just two-thirds of its present workforce. Procter & Gamble, with sales rising, is dismissing 12 percent of its employees. Manufacturing is not alone in downsizing: Cigna Reinsurance, an arm of the Philadelphia giant, has trimmed its workforce 25 percent since 1990. Global competition has accelerated sharply in just the past few years. The market value of U.S. direct investment abroad rose 35 percent to $776 billion from 1987 to 1992, while the value of foreign direct investment in America more than doubled to $692 billion. The revolution in information technology is creating tools that permit just such agility. The next trend is companies that empower their customers.

As the usefulness of information, information technology, and information work grows, businesses find more ways to substitute them for expensive investments in physical assets, such as factories, warehouses, and inventories. Buildings and stockpiles—physical assets—have been replaced by networks and databases—intellectual assets.[22]

The era of revolutionary corporate change promises enormous economic improvements at an exceptionally high cost in human pain. Companies must transform themselves radically to survive and become more competitive. One result is structural change in the labor market, with downsizing continuing even in a period of economic recovery.

STRATEGIC AND SOCIETAL CONSEQUENCES

Companies can cause stress to workers who merely fear losing their jobs or who cannot navigate new organization structures or handle their new responsibilities. The only way to deal with twenty direct reports, for example, is to delegate more, but many veteran managers seem unable to let go. Job-related suicides are up, along with employee violence, ranging from sabotage of computer systems to bloody rampages with assault weapons.

How will society handle such dilemmas, as competition forces businesses into radical change? This workplace revolution may be remembered as a historic event. But, as corporations abandon the unwritten contract of lifetime employment in return for hard work and loyalty, the social fabric of the United States seems weaker than at any point in the postwar years. Is America up to the challenges that it must face?

Once the organization is flattened, and workers are empowered, shared values provide the only practical way to ensure that everyone is aimed in the same direction. Corporate values such as candor, integrity, facing reality, taking responsibility, being accountable, investing in education, and respecting diversity sound good, but are they really being applied and practiced in a way that makes the organization more effective?

The turmoil in the workplace results in part from management ineffectiveness that made these organizations less competitive. Workers who gave loyalty under the old system have suffered under the new. It is no surprise that employee cynicism has grown.[23]

For effective change to occur, even in large organizations, which depend on thousands of employees understanding the company, strategies must be translated into appropriate actions and leaders must win over their followers one by one.

The problem for most executives is that managing change is unlike any other managerial task they have ever confronted. An organization may simultaneously be working on total quality management (TQM), process reengineering, employee empowerment, and several other programs designed to improve performance. In managing change, the key goal is understanding how pieces balance off one another, how changing one element changes the rest, how sequencing and pace affect the whole structure.

One tool that companies can use to provide that critical balance is the *Change Management Team,* a group of company leaders, reporting to the CEO, who commit all their time and energy to managing the change process. When that process has stabilized, the CMT disbands and then oversees the corporate change effort. Managing change means improving the communication between the people leading the change effort and those who are expected to implement the new strategies, managing the organizational context in which change can occur.

When managers or CMT members put off communicating with the rest of the organization, they prevent people from understanding the design principles that guided them and the lessons they learned from previous experience. They unwittingly prevent the people who are expected to implement the change from participating or buying in. As a consequence, no matter how good the new design turns out to be, it does not produce the expected results.

Everything managers say, how they act, or listen, sends a message. Many managers assume that communication is a staff function, a job for human resources or public relations. In fact, communication during the reengineering process must be a priority for every manager at every level of the company. People in the organization may need to hear a message over and over before they believe that, this time, the call for change is not just this year's "hula hoop" or whim. It takes time for people to hear, understand, and believe the message.

The old management paradigm said that at work, people are only permitted to feel emotions that are easily controllable, emotions that can be categorized as positive. The new management paradigm says that managing people is managing feelings.

The CEO's job is to be a visible champion for the transformation, articulating the context and rationale for the new corporate direction. This means having a clear understanding of the long-term vision of the company.[24]

People who are organizationally codependent have enabled the system to control their sense of worth and self-esteem, at the same time investing tremendous energy attempting to control the system. Honest companies will avoid encouraging such codependency.[25]

Dynamic Growth

Traditionally, in business, managers added production capacity, allowed overhead to swell, and stockpiled inventories in anticipation of rising demand during expansions. When the economy declined, they shut factories, laid off workers, cancelled new product development, and purged excess inventories at distress prices. The result was that profits vanished as high fixed costs had to be spread over a smaller sales base.

The best strategy to avoid this cycle and to succeed in a downturn is to beat the competitors to the market through dynamic growth. Black & Decker has speeded up the development process by organizing teams of design engineers, production managers, and marketers to work on an entire family of new products from its inception. The team, using an approach called concurrent engineering, looks for ways to standardize components across several new products to make them easier and less costly to assemble.[26]

Achieving profitable growth is harder than cutting costs. Unlike raising profits by shrinking expenses, increasing revenue through product innovation or geographical expansion requires managers to have a vision about where technology is going, how markets can be developed, what consumers will want, where your industry is moving, and how you can move with it—or ahead of it. Cutting and reengineering are only part of the mission because restructuring has to have a commitment to growth.

In China, reengineering is the reverse of what is seen in the United States. There, it is not characterized by downsizing, but by dynamic growth, since China is experiencing almost unpredictable growth and business organizations have to change rapidly to adjust to market challenges.[27]

Growth managers need to reconceive their business entirely, not just improve it incrementally at the edges. They need the ability to break the rules, to be able to think outside the box and go beyond the established parameters of how things in the organization were previously done. It is important for managers and employees to develop a mentality that identifies real problems in their business dealings and to find new, creative solutions. The people who go through restructuring and downsizing without a plan of growth are like the people who consume assets rather than invest in them.[28]

The most profound way of thinking about reengineering comes from Joseph Schumpeter, one of the greatest economists, more than fifty years ago. The essential feature of the capitalist system, Schumpeter said, was "creative destruction," which he defined as "an organic process of industrial mutation that incessantly revolutionizes the economic structure *from within*, incessantly destroying the old one, incessantly creating a new one" (emphasis added).[29]

CASE STUDY

Com Company Case

Jason Roberts has worked for Com Company for nineteen years and experienced three downsizing efforts in his departments. Advances in technology and a highly competitive global marketplace required his company to change to become more competitive. Change is a necessary part of his business. In Jason's first two corporate downsizing experiences, he worked in another department, and his previous boss did not openly and effectively communicate the reason for the downsizing, creating morale problems within the department. Four months ago, Jason's present department downsized its staff. However, his current boss made an unpleasant experience *not* unpleasant by openly and honestly communicating the entire downsizing process. As a result, there was no morale problem and the fear of losing one's job was never an issue. Jason's title is Director of Operations, Receivables Management—New York State, for Com Company. He operates a 1,000 person call center (three different locations—Brooklyn, Manhattan, and Syracuse) that speaks with residential customers regarding delinquent payments. Their hours of operation are Monday through Saturday, 8:00 a.m. to 9:00 p.m. All of their measurements are calculated on a monthly basis. Jason is responsible for collecting $51 million per month, achieving an 85 percent service level (85 percent of incoming calls answered within twenty seconds), and other customer service indicators such as Public Service Commission complaints and customer satisfaction surveys.

Since Jason is responsible for balancing all of these measures, having one of the time frames of these measures cut in half would have a tremendous downstream effect on his organization. If he took dollars collected, for example, and was told to collect $51 million in two weeks as opposed to one month, many things would fall by the wayside.

First, their commitment to the regulators that they answer 85 percent of their calls within twenty seconds would be virtually unattainable. Jason would need to forego that objective and concentrate heavily on a proactive outbound dialing campaign to reach enough customers. Public Service Commission complaints would increase as well.

Second, intuitively, Jason thinks their commitment to excellent customer service would temporarily go out the window. They would be talking to too many customers, too aggressively, and he feels that would have an adverse effect on their customer service results. Employees would feel the squeeze as well because they would need to impose mandatory overtime to get through the work.

Do you have any recommendations how Jason Roberts can institute some effective change efforts regarding his concerns and circumstances at Com Company?

Chapter 2

Reengineering's Consequences

INTRODUCTION

Legitimate reengineering is a matter of streamlining internal processes and eliminating redundancies—which is threatening enough to managers who may already feel rendered obsolete by automation and employee empowerment. But reengineering has also become a euphemism for any kind of staff reduction or de-layering. A study of several dozen Fortune 500 companies strongly suggests that continued bouts of reorganization actually have a deleterious effect on performance.[1]

Facing complex and often intractable problems, companies choose time and again to reorganize, each time hoping that they will finally get it right. The data are clear and suggest that these reengineering efforts do not always work. The implications of the findings are twofold: one should think long and hard before reorganizing to make sure that the cure matches the disease. Many executives reach for the reengineering option first because it is something within their control. A study by Arthur D. Little found that nearly 85 percent of executives were dissatisfied with their reengineering results, and many viewed the strategy as a euphemism for downsizing.[2]

CEOs should keep in mind that all reengineering, whether launched for the right or wrong reasons, can put a company into shock. Reengineering can also tend to bring out people's ambition and competitiveness, which can amplify already existing interpersonal tensions. The decision to reorganize, the research suggests, is one that managers need to approach with great trepidation.[3]

Today's managers are faced with more pressure than their predecessors because of how much is expected of them, such as slashed budgets, downsized workforces, mergers, and acquisitions. With downsizing and cost cutting in recent years, people feel more stress because they do not view their jobs as stable. (See Table 2.1 for some consequences of reengineering efforts.)

TABLE 2.1. The Aftermath of Reengineering

- 3.4 million jobs cut by Fortune 500 Firms/20 percent middle management.
- Consolidated job and management duties.
- Talent pool of top executives is shallow.
- Performance results scrutinized more harshly.
- Firms are unwilling to fill positions based on potential.
- Flat career growth patterns.
- Need for personal job restructuring.
- With available positions higher salaries and bonuses.
- More time devoted to find top talent.
- Law of diminishing returns/what's the payoff?
- Morale issues for survivors.
- Emphasis on outsourcing.

THE HUMAN SIDE OF REENGINEERING

Job Stress/Burnout

According to the 1996 *Yankelovich Monitor,* an annual report published by the Norwalk, Connecticut-based, market research firm Yankelovich Partners, 33 percent of all Americans believe their jobs are more stressful than a year ago. In addition, the American Institute of Stress reports that 78 percent of Americans describe their jobs as stressful, with more than two-thirds stating that the situation has become worse in the last five years.[4]

The condition of burnout occurs after prolonged periods of unrelenting stress on the job. The inability to gain control causes employees to feel unable to cope with the high demands of their job. Job burnout is characterized by feelings of hopelessness and thoughts of leaving or withdrawing from work. Burned-out workers feel demoralized, and their job loses meaning for them.

In job burnout, workers lack energy and motivation. Their productivity plummets, and they often suffer from insomnia, headaches, backaches, and other ailments. They work longer and harder, but never seem to catch up. They can turn to alcohol, drugs, or other addictive behavior. In today's world of layoffs, reengineered organizations, two-income families, and fierce global competition, a veritable epidemic of job stress has continued, even after the recession of the early 1990s had ended.

In a 1993 survey of 3,400 workers by the Families and Work Institute, a nonprofit research organization, 42 percent reported feeling burned out or "used up" at the end of the workday, 80 percent said they had to work very hard, and 65 percent said they had to work very fast.

Research has shown that stress is clearly linked to burnout. A 1992 survey of 1,300 workers by the ReliaStar Insurance Company of Minneapolis found that employees who felt their jobs were highly stressful were twice as likely to experience burnout than those who did not find their work stressful. At highest risk were low-income workers, especially those with college degrees, and single mothers.

A 1992 survey of 28,000 workers by St. Paul Fire & Marine, for instance, found four major problems that lead to job burnout: (1) poor supervision, including a supervisor who is critical, expects too much, is not open to discussing problems, organizes departmental work poorly, and does not recognize employees for a job well done; (2) lack of teamwork, including tension and bad feelings within a work group and a failure to pitch in when needed; (3) unreasonable workload, including employees who feel overworked, can't meet deadlines, and can't keep up with changes; (4) unfair company practices, including promotions that are perceived as unjust and discrimination on the basis of race, sex, or age.

According to the American Institute of Stress, job stress and burnout cost employers an estimated $200 billion a year in turnover costs, absenteeism, lower productivity, and rising worker's compensation and health care claims. The research found that companies with supportive work and family policies, health coverage for mental illness and chemical dependency treatment, effective communication, and flexible work hours had nearly half the burnout rate of employers who did not have such policies.[5]

According to data by the American Management Association (AMA), every year since 1988, at least one-third, and sometimes more than one-half, of large and midsize U.S. companies have downsized their workforces. Once content to trim mostly hourly workers, employers are now targeting managers and professionals in unprecedented numbers. But just where is all this cutting leading? Only 34 percent of these companies reported any increases in productivity to the AMA, and only 45 percent have seen their operating profits improve. In addition, two-thirds of corporations that reduce their ranks in one year, follow up with another round of cuts the next, reports the AMA. A distressing 80 percent of downsizers admit that the morale of their remaining employees has been lowered. Unfortunately, these demoralized employees are supposed to revitalize the organization and delight customers.[6]

In an era beset by unending restructuring, sometimes driven demandingness can be downright abusive. Such bosses often do whatever works without looking at the consequences of their behavior on other people. The abusive boss is constantly angry with himself or herself and others for falling short of his or her ideal.[7] Personal problems such as alcoholism and depression are common among the newly unemployed, and marriages are often strained. Much stress must be dealt with, including family stress.

For many, the years ahead are shaping up as the Age of Job Stress. To white-collar workers who have lost their jobs and are struggling to find a new foothold, it is a bitter irony: the survivors of mergers, downsizings, leveraged buyouts (LBOs), and recession-induced cost cutting may hope for more balance in their lives, but they are too worried about holding on to their place in the company to do anything about those dreams.

Increased Workload

Anecdotal evidence and survey data strongly suggest that many white-collar Americans are approaching the Japanese tradition of twelve-hour days and work-filled evenings. Priority Management, a Seattle consulting firm, recently polled 1,344 middle managers on a variety of topics and reported that the number of hours people said they are working was the study's "single most startling finding." Although about one-third work forty to forty-five hours weekly, 57 percent are routinely at their desks from six to twenty hours more than that, and 6 percent say they work upward of sixty hours.

Putting in longer hours does not necessarily ensure that the job gets done. A separate study by the American Management Association showed that 41 percent of middle managers say they have more work than time to do it. This helps explain why the Priority Management survey found that 85 percent of managers worry about how to lead a more balanced life, with time for family, hobbies, and volunteer work. Only one in fifty claims success at juggling everything.

A survey of white-collar workers in 1,005 companies found that 86 percent of their employers had done a major restructuring, or more than one, in the preceding five years. About 66 percent of the people surveyed believe that their new, heavier workload is reasonable. The definition of reasonable is shifting, and managers are accepting tougher demands as a way of life.

The American Management Association study reported on how pressed for time everyone feels these days. Nearly half the managers who responded said they sometimes, or often, work harder and longer to escape pressures in other areas of their lives—trouble at home, for instance.

In today's leaner organizations, managers have the feeling that if they keep meeting their goals, senior-level management will keep setting them higher. Since managers react so differently to stress, it is hard to generalize about what is "overwork." One person's exhilarating schedule is another's intolerable grind.

In Japan, whose work ethic U.S. companies seem increasingly eager to emulate, the phenomenon of *karoshi* is well-known. The word means "death by overwork," usually from a heart attack, and the key to it is not hours put in, but the attitude of the worker. The health risks of hating one's job have been known to medical researchers in the United States since 1972, when a Massachusetts study showed that the surest predictor of heart disease was not smoking, cholesterol, or lack of exercise, but job dissatisfaction.[8]

Expecting managers to meet unrealistically high goals can lead to cheating, as people struggle to make their numbers look good. The greatest cost to corporations of stressing out managers over long periods of time is also the most ineffable. It is impossible to say how much better a company might be doing if its managers were not quite so busy or quite so tired. How many bad decisions might be avoided? How many innovative ideas might never have a chance to bloom? Similar to generalized stress, burnout cuts across executive and managerial levels. Although the phenomenon manifests itself in varying ways and to different degrees in different people, it appears, nonetheless, to have identifiable characteristics.

People suffering from burnout generally have certain identifiable characteristics, such as (1) chronic fatigue; (2) anger at those making demands; (3) self-criticism for putting up with the demands; (4) cynicism, negativity, and irritability; (5) a sense of being besieged; and (6) hair-trigger display of emotions. Burned-out managers may inappropriately vent anger at subordinates and family or withdraw, even from those whose support they need the most. They may try to escape the source of pressure through illness, absenteeism, or drugs or alcohol or by seeking temporary psychological refuge in meditation, biofeedback, or other forms of self-hypnosis. In addition, they may display increasingly rigid attitudes or appear cold and detached.

It is essential for an organization to have a systematic way of letting people know that their contributions are important. People need information that supports their positive self-image, eases their conscience, and refuels them psychologically. Many compensation and performance appraisal programs actually contribute to people's sense that their efforts will be unrecognized no matter how well they do. Organizational structures and processes that inhibit timely attacks on problems and delay competitive actions can produce much of the stress that people feel at work. If managers fail to see that organizational factors can cause burnout, their lack of understanding may perpetuate the problem. -

Managers should provide avenues through which people can express not only their anger but also their disappointment, helplessness, hopelessness, defeat, and depression. Top management needs to retrain, refresh, and reinvigorate these managers as quickly as possible by encouraging them to attend seminars, workshops, and other activities away from the organization. Reengineering, downsizing, and increased competition have multiplied these pressures in the workplace.[9]

Uncertain Futures

A survey of about 1,000 readers by *Industry Week* magazine reported that 60 percent of middle managers say they are less loyal to their employers than five years ago. Another study, by the management consulting firm Hay Group, says that in 1979 almost three-quarters of middle managers were optimistic about their chances for advancement. By the end of 1987, mainly because of layoffs and restructurings they had seen, only about one-third still thought their futures looked favorable.[10] A new Census Bureau report showing that the average income of households earning over $100,000 declined 7 percent between 1989 and 1992, after adjusting for inflation.

Parents also worry about the future their children may face because the job market has become increasingly competitive. Feelings of guilt from all the hours away from home are already exerting their influence. The proportion of working women who would rather stay home climbed to 53 percent in 1992 from 43 percent in 1985, a dramatic reversal of the move toward more involvement in work that started in the early 1970s. According to a 1991 study, half of working mothers and 40 percent of fathers have considered cutting back to create more family time.[11]

NEW RULES IN THE BUSINESS ENVIRONMENT

The Bureau of Labor Statistics forecasts that the economy will add some 1.7 million new jobs each year from now to 2005. Only one-third will come from Fortune 500 companies. To retool for global competition, businesses must reallocate money to capital investment. Consequently, companies have cut their debt burdens sharply since 1989, making themselves more attractive to investors.

The growth of productivity and compensation first parted company in the early 1980s, when U.S. manufacturers pared their ranks in response to fierce foreign competition. Workers lost more bargaining power when the service sector—home to 75 percent of nongovernmental employees—computerized and contracted to meet competitive challenges. Table 2.2 shows the changes in the marketplace that have created a more volatile business environment and the need for reengineering as a management tool, as well as the skill base that managers and employees need.

TABLE 2.2. Marketplace/Volatile Business Environment Characteristics

Changes	Change Outcome	Skill Base
Technology		Computer/Internet
Globalization		Global understanding
Quality levels/TQM	Reengineering	Error-free service
Greater customer demands		Customer relationship building
		Quantitative ability
Higher business costs		Core competencies
Competitive environment		Managing a diverse workplace
Demographic realities		

No wonder the boss looks strangely at employees who have the temerity to ask for a raise. As companies across the country now realize, the new economy is fundamentally changing the rules and rewards of the workplace. Though people may work harder, and smarter, raises will not automatically follow as they once did. The challenge facing bosses is to find new ways to hang on to valued employees.[12]

"For at least twelve to eighteen months, management has been trying to deliver the message that we're growing again," says Jerome Colletti, President of The Alexander Group, Incorporated, a Stamford, Connecticut, consulting firm. Naturally, sales and marketing teams regard themselves as the people who actually make the growth happen. Colletti says, "The salespeople have demonstrated that they are the competitive advantage and they're gonna put the moves on you" in terms of higher pay.

Management Skill Base

The Association of Executive Search Consultants reports that searches for general managers below the division-head level increased 58 percent last year. The skills needed to succeed in those positions have changed considerably during the 1990s (see Figure 2.1). In today's business environment, middle managers who cannot add sub-

FIGURE 2.1. Percentage of Managers Who Felt More Problems Were Created in Their Organizations by Reengineering

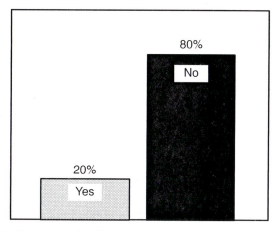

80%

No

20%

Yes

Source: Carter Reengineering Survey (1998).

stantive value to the organization are candidates for extinction. GE went from seven layers of management to three during the decade ending in 1995. In enlightened organizations, middle-level managers are viewed as valuable commodities, well positioned to serve not only as interpreters and conduits but as shapers and drivers of corporate strategy. At one time, they may have supervised ten people. Today, they must win the support of employees of different backgrounds, job titles, and cultures. Also, these new managers are expected to be skilled at organizing complex subjects, solving problems, communicating ideas, and making swift decisions.

Today's managers need a broader knowledge of their industry, as well as of every corner of their own organizations. The trait CEOs say they want their managers to possess, above all others, more than *any* functional skill, is leadership. Leaders have a charisma that challenges their subordinates to achieve their very best. They impart a vision that makes people believe and want to follow them.

America's largest companies, on the whole, have not been job creators for years. The Fortune 500 industrial firms have cut more jobs since 1982 (2.6 million) than the Service 500 have added (2.1 million).[13]

The ranks of the discouraged are loaded with older workers, especially those past fifty-five. According to a survey conducted by the Commonwealth Fund, a New York research group, at least 2 million older workers are ready and able to work, but cannot find jobs. A recent Conference Board survey of 400 big companies found about 40 percent offering early retirement packages as part of downsizing efforts.

Advocates for older workers say that attitude is not just cruel but also downright stupid. The Conference Board study found that companies continue to lay off and package out senior workers even though they are more reliable than younger employees, have better work attitudes, have better job skills, are absent less often, and are less likely to quit. About 70 percent of the companies surveyed also said older workers were at least as cost-effective as their younger colleagues. In a survey of 376 unemployed executives conducted by the New York City outplacement firm Lee Hecht Harrison, 90 percent said they needed to upgrade their abilities, particularly communication skills, before even entering the interview circuit.[14]

Downsizing

The terms downsizing and right-sizing, suggesting a one-time correction, have become passé. The big shrink at large manufacturing and service companies has less to do with tepid economic recovery in the United States and recessions in major export markets than with deep structural changes. The new mind-set among job-cutting companies is that the world economy faces a sustained period of slow, low-inflationary expansion and global overcapacity, an era in which they cannot easily raise prices to expand profit margins. Every day it becomes clearer that layoffs, 1990s style, are unlike those of the past. In the 1980s, employers used layoffs as a blunt instrument to cut costs. They shed employees to reap one-time, often transitory, savings. As business picked up, or as management began to hope it would, many companies would start hiring again. Full-time workers who were laid off in the 1990s suffered an average earnings loss of 10 percent upon rehire. This is because large companies have cut more jobs that pay above the industry average than they have created. Smaller businesses have created more jobs than they have eliminated at all pay levels, but many have done so at reduced compensation for comparable skills. As a result of this wage erosion, the unemployed or reemployed who are trying to maintain their former lifestyles have increased borrowing, relying on previously established lines of credit.[15]

Layoffs, the inevitable by-product of the new drive for cost-lowering efficiencies, may ultimately render big companies more fit to combat tenacious global competitors. The questions that remain unanswered are "Will they ever begin to create jobs in significant numbers and where are the displaced employees to find work?"[16]

Companies that once bragged about their reengineered work processes and new quality measurements now are extolling the importance of human beings. They want to hire them, retain them, develop them, and pay them gobs of money. Many companies are spotlighting managers to help rebuild cultures disrupted by mergers and cost cutting and to appear people friendly in an era of labor shortages. Concurrently, companies cannot seem to find enough people with all the qualities they want. In a nationwide survey of 1,000 executives by Caliper, a human resources consulting firm based in Princeton, New Jersey, 25 percent of employers said they frequently hire people who lack the qualities they want, such as problem-solving skills and conscientiousness. Companies want committed workers who can tackle tough problems; employees want security and stability, a chance to do interesting work, a boss they like and respect, and good pay and benefits.[17]

Flex Time

The rate of shift-schedule changes is accelerating as plants and factories switch to twenty-four-hour, seven-day operation and streamline shift schedules to raise their returns. Many are switching to twelve-hour from eight-hour shifts and replacing fixed shifts with rotating ones. The goal is to distribute skilled employees evenly among shifts and ease communication between shift workers and day management. Employers lay out basic requirements such as hours of operation, distribution of skilled workers among shifts, number of time-eating shift turnovers a day, employee availability for training, and so on. They educate workers about the physiological and social effects of shift-schedule alternatives, then let the workers vote. The result is often a schedule that is better for everyone. Involving employees in picking shift schedules is not easy, since the process never yields consensus. Workers' individual lives and preferences are just too diverse, and deciding on a new schedule always raises powerful emotions, even if a majority agrees.[18]

Globalization

More and more Americans are sharing a global job market with counterparts who work for far less. A fundamental shift is under way in how and where the world's work gets done—with potentially ominous consequences for wealthy, industrialized nations. The key to this change is the emergence of a truly global labor force that is talented and capable of accomplishing just about anything, anywhere. This truly competitive global workforce is vying for industrial nations' jobs. The rest of the world is catching up.

Just what is driving U.S. companies—and some from Europe and Japan—to locate their new plants in Bangalore, India, or Guadalajara, Mexico? It is not only the search for cheap labor. Corporations also want to establish sophisticated manufacturing and service operations in markets that promise the most growth, often emerging nations. The migration of jobs to new lands is not a straightforward one-for-one proposition either—one job gained there for every one lost to the industrialized country. Profitability, at the expense of downgrading the productivity of all key resources and not innovating, destroys capital.[19] New technology and the continuing drive for higher productivity push companies to build in undeveloped countries plants and offices that require only a fraction of the manpower that used to be needed in factories back home. If companies reduce 1 million jobs at home through reengineering their work, they may add many overseas.[20]

CASE STUDY

Dublin Incorporated

Today, critical projects and subprojects are an everyday reality in any company. The securities industry is constantly placing demands on Dublin Incorporated, a securities brokerage firm, to perform systems enhancements and to take the lead in the industry's year 2000 conversion problem, which is now collectively known as the Y2K endeavor.

As a developer, Jill Barker was recently handed a project to create a database to support her department's vice president, who was recently appointed, in Dublin Incorporated, as Chairman of the Exchange and Utilities Committee (E & U). The E & U consists of all the stock exchanges and clearing houses in the United States and Canada. Her VP, Mr. Romano, chairs a monthly meeting of the E & U Committee. These meetings can be tense and heated because each entity inevitably is in pursuit of its own agenda. Despite the formidable task facing Mr. Romano, he handles all "crises" with skill and decorum. Albeit, Mr. Romano cannot maintain cohesion and direction alone. He depends on the team effort of his staff. Like a presidential entourage, Mr. Romano's team has to provide all the industry participants' with daily changes and developments that have to be current and accurate.

It is against this backdrop that Jill has about a month to develop and create a database of all the key players, with over 800 participant companies, for example, brokerage houses (Merrill Lynch, Lehman Brothers, etc.), banks (Citibank, Chase, etc.), exchanges and utilities (NYSE, AMEX, NSCC, etc.).

How can Jill handle this project and avoid burnout for her and her staff?

SECTION II:
PRACTICAL OUTCOMES

Chapter 3

Urgency Theory

INTRODUCTION

Middle-level managers' jobs are vanishing in mergers, takeovers, and restructurings, or management vogues are radically altering their traditional roles. Yet getting those middle-level managers to embrace a new corporate vision is the most important step and greatest challenge when a large company tries to reform itself. Middle-level managers are often directly on the firing line when a company begins experimenting with a new management method. They are asked to learn entirely different ways of behaving, and their worth to the company can suddenly depend on their ability or willingness to change. The pressures can be intense, leading at times to a kind of professional identity crisis.

Reengineering implies the need to restructure due to changes in the business environment. It means having a system or process for success. In making changes, the use of teams provides different perspective and opportunities. There also must be an organizational commitment to the company's core values. Having the ability to establish results and developing success initiatives is important to justify the risks taken when engaging in a reengineering process. It also instills confidence in the staff and gets them to "buy in" to the process. Identifying the resources for changes that determine the transition to the new culture will also be helpful.

Most companies downsize without figuring out how to reduce the workload. Even at companies with no immediate plans to let anybody go, fear is endemic. Companies that have cut personnel and assigned extra work to the survivors should now devote themselves to figuring out what really does need to be done and what does not.

The issue of *doing more with less* is an example of a practical application that results from reengineering (see Figure 3.1). Some of the answers to this dilemma may be found by doing *different* with less. This can involve eliminating unproductive methods, avoiding duplication, increasing performance, retaining good employees, and incorporating technology. Other answers can come from effective cost containment, tracking sound outcomes assessment, and considering the ideal of paradigm shift instead of achieving short-term goals. To develop a system or process for success, ask which costs are contributing to what the company does and wants to accomplish to know what to eliminate. The opportunity costs that determine what is lost or gained in cost by doing something a particular way should also be examined. A line manager may be concerned that if he or she is able to save budget dollars for the company, he or she will lose those dollars in next year's budget, but the focus should be how to do a better job with less money. Some alternatives to these changes are increased workloads, the use of part-timers, and fewer support staff.

FIGURE 3.1. Percentage of Organizations That Faced Situations of "Doing More with Less" Due to Reengineering

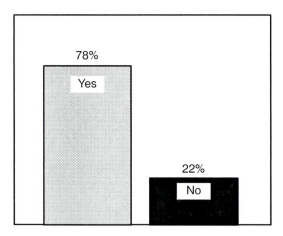

Source: Carter Reengineering Survey (1998).

EFFECTIVE REENGINEERING

Managers should make a case for action, establish a positive vision of the future, focus on a few mission-critical processes, and involve customers and outside constituencies in the reengineering effort. They should also target broad changes in business strategy, set clear, measurable goals, and empower employees to perform while implementing. Last, demand senior management leadership, look for early wins, and remember that not all business processes require radical redesign.

Middle-level managers and midlevel supervisors are expected to empower lower-level employees, to nurture their talents and draw out their ideas, and to do it all without harsh criticism. Eliminating some middle managers gives those remaining new freedom to do their jobs. Xerox decided a few years ago to cut back on headquarters staff who had been overseeing the work of district supervisors and to greatly increase the power of managers in the field. District managers suddenly had far more authority to adjust prices or to extend credit to valued customers. As long as expected results are achieved, corporate-level managers stay away. Top executives must arm middle managers with detailed information on their status and the company's prospects. Concealing the truth about future changes only fuels anxiety, rumors, and resentment. Midlevel supervisors, if fully acquainted with details of changes in the works, can quell discontent, and if they know their role in the new plan, they can also help persuade the rank and file to accept it.

Middle-level managers need to be far more flexible than before, yet many companies make the mistake of pigeonholing supervisors according to their technical skills, failing to nurture their general management abilities. Often the result is a core group of supervisors far too narrowly focused on the details of their jobs. One way to get supervisors thinking in broader terms is to make sure they are exposed to a variety of jobs. Realigning people forces them to develop new skills and recognize the linkages between seemingly disparate parts of the enterprise. The supervisor, once involved solely in some aspect of production and now well acquainted with the budgetary process or marketing problems, will likely be a far more valuable employee. The volatile trends that have shaken U.S.

corporations will continue or accelerate in coming years. Global competition is certain to intensify, requiring fresh thinking about how to manage.[1]

Reengineering is based on the concept of significantly altering existing models and thinking and using dramatic improvements that are accomplished by reinventing the way in which work is done. It is characterized as the radical redesign of an organization's business processes to achieve strategic breakthroughs. Volatile business conditions have driven the use of reengineering and have led to drastic corporate downsizing, meaning organizations are expected to do more with less. Some reengineering efforts have shown remarkable results. For example, following reengineering, from 1993 to 1995, sales per employee at Huls America increased 38 percent and operating income, 48 percent. Huls redefined its business in 1993 by generating sales of about $200 million and cutting about 20 percent in overhead.[2]

However, has reengineering accomplished its objective of breakthrough results and huge advances in performance? Findings based on research conducted with ninety-two Fortune 500 companies that have used reengineering suggest that most organizations are not always significantly effective due to difficulties in handling the time management aspects resulting from a reengineering effort.

APPLYING URGENCY THEORY

The "doing more with less" aspect to reengineering means time resource management problems arise from reengineering efforts. Obtaining greater productivity and performance from employees in significantly less time is a constant management concern. *Urgency theory* involves organizations dealing with the phenomenon of "doing more with less" that results from a reengineering effort.[3] It challenges a manager's ability to effectively manage time pressure, limited resources, and fewer people after reengineering, while trying to augment productivity and performance output. To be able to assign half the time to their subordinates to complete a task/project, what would managers do differently, how would they handle the process, and what would they cut out? In effect, this goes beyond an abstract time and resource management question, but it has a practical application to what reengineering creates when downsizing occurs.

:

As an example, time-pressured performance results that have intensified from reengineering have particular relevance to sales organizations. If a sales department was downsized from sixteen salespeople to nine, then what is essentially expected of them is time urgency, or doing more with less.

Urgency Theory

How do you effectively manage the time management aspects of what's left from a reengineering effort?

For example, if you had half the time to get something accomplished (urgency theory), how would you handle the process? What would you do differently? What would you cut out?

So, from a productivity standpoint, managers should emphasize the use of time management principles to maximize desired favorable results from reengineering. For example, would the sales force more effectively target accounts with greater revenue potential, communicate better within the organization, rely more heavily on technology, such as e-mail, or schedule meetings only when necessary? The average salesperson spends forty-seven hours a week at work, but only fourteen hours per week are spent directly selling to clients. The flexible work hours and lack of a typical workday for salespeople makes their use of time management skills essential, especially with a reengineered sales force.

Urgency Theory—Relevance to Sales Organizations

Average salesperson spends forty-seven hours a week at work. Only fourteen hours per week are spent selling.

The competitive message that times have changed has created much stress in the business environment. Both global and domestic competition and the emphasis on speeding up work and lowering costs has forced many corporations to become leaner. A New York firm that surveys employee attitudes for corporations has reviewed the responses of over 1 million employees at 171 large corporations over the past eighteen years. These findings have shown that the number of managers who say they have too much to do has jumped from 34 percent to 46 percent in the past five years. In addition, 40 percent of nonmanagers say they have too much work also, compared with 30 percent previously. Getting the most out of employees without pushing them too hard needs to be an ongoing process. For example, a Gallup survey of personnel and medical directors at 200 large and small corporations revealed that, on average, 25 percent of their companies' employees suffered from anxiety or stress-related disorders. In many instances, these stressed employees missed sixteen days of work per year. In addition, job stress disorders, along with job-related substance abuse, cost the United States annually, in lost productivity, job errors, and doctors' bills, $183 billion.[4]

Management should look for solutions to the consequences of reengineering. Corporate restructuring and reengineering have dictated the need for organizations to accomplish more tasks in the same amount of time. This phenomenon is the essence of urgency theory (see Table 3.1 for advantages and disadvantages of applying

TABLE 3.1. Urgency Theory—Advantages and Disadvantages

Advantages

- Greater productivity and performance in less time
- Identifies salespeople who can respond to urgent demands
- Greater customer responsiveness and appreciation of customers' time needs
- Significant competitive advantage
- Improved ability to develop innovations and more core competencies
- Eliminates weak performers
- Better time management

Disadvantages

- Not everyone can operate effectively under urgent demands
- Morale problems from feeling pressure
- Quality levels, mistakes, and inefficiencies from haste
- Possible inattentiveness to customers
- Need for technology tools for support
- Causes chaos
- Burnout factor
- Too many responsibilities
- Doing more with less

this theory). Given the aftermath of reengineering, time has become an even greater critical source of competitive advantage and a strategic tool with value comparable to many business resources, such as revenue, speed, efficiency, and quality. Accordingly, managers must emphasize efficient productive time and resource management. To be results oriented and to generate effective performance means recognizing that the return on invested time is as important as the return on invested money. An effective time management device for managers is to avoid being surprised and to use anticipatory action. This forces the use of effective planning, which results in deliberate objective and priority setting that gives managers and subordinates an order of sequential action steps to follow.

Comparative Advantage

Comparative advantage, which says that each person should do the work he or she is best qualified for, is another tool in the aftermath of reengineering that can help managers assign responsibilities to subordinates commensurate with their expertise. Delegation, as a management skill, is an additional tool available to managers that can help with the time urgency that has resulted from reengineering. Delegating managers should ask the following questions:

- Can someone else perform this task better than I can?
- Can someone else perform this task at a lower cost than I can?
- Is work being delegated in a manner that takes full advantage of the knowledge, background, and experience level of the employees?

When managers delegate tasks, it provides, along with time management guidelines, empowerment and job enrichment and produces better morale, reduced turnover, and increased initiative. Last, the "doing more with less" aspects of reengineering can benefit from the use of team building within the organization. This can contribute to efficient time production, lower costs, and speed up the time frame required to launch new products and services.

Improved Efficiency

Reengineering, as a management tool, should be aimed at creating trimmer, more focused organizations with reinvigorated sales activity. The aftermath of reengineering has instead resulted in additional time burdens for managers and employees who are denied the opportunity to maximize their performance capability.[5]

Successful businesses are those which evolve rapidly and effectively. Yet innovative businesses can not evolve in a vacuum. They must attract resources of all sorts, drawing in capital, partners, suppliers, and customers to create cooperative networks. In essence, executives must develop new ideas and tools for strategizing, tools for making tough choices related to innovations, business alliances, and leadership of customers and suppliers. A business ecosystem, similar to its biological counterpart, gradually moves from a random collection of elements to a more structured community.

Every business ecosystem develops in four distinct stages: birth, expansion, leadership, and self-renewal—or, if not self-renewal, death. In reality, of course, the evolutionary stages blur, and the managerial challenges of one stage often crop up in another. What remains the same from business to business is the process of coevolution, which is, the complex interplay between competitive and cooperative business strategies.[6]

According to an annual report that tracks consumer values and lifestyle choices, one-third of all Americans report that their jobs are more stressful than a year ago. That same study found that 75 percent of Americans believe their lives are too complicated—in 1985, only 50 percent of Americans felt that way. Furthermore, nearly half of all U.S. businesses have cut back on their workforces in the past ten years, and compared to 1985 workloads, the average employee does the work of 1.3 people.

For example, sales and marketing professionals are by no means average employees. They probably do the work of three or four people. They are constantly being asked to do sixty hours of work in a forty-hour week. In addition to the classic time wasters—meetings, paperwork, evaluations—that are deemed necessary by bureaucratic institutions, managers must accomplish those tasks which actually bring value to their organizations: assisting representatives on sales calls, forecasting, and training. Combined with family obligations, the daily planner becomes a painful reminder of what they did not accomplish. By pushing themselves to accomplish more, they are actually being counterproductive. Considering the shift in corporate America toward globalization, reengineering, and downsizing, this newfound pressure is understandable.[7]

The demand for flexible job arrangements was ranked highest among the employees companies can least afford to lose: those who worked long hours, were very committed to their jobs, and had the most sophisticated skills. The reluctance of some companies to use flexible job arrangements is inconsistent with being output driven. Most managers equate presence at the office with productivity, but this is not always a valid conclusion. Studies show that the productivity of workers who have control over where, when, or how long they work *exceeds* that of employees who work a standard shift at the office. Companies committed to a nine-to-five mentality are augmenting worker stress and hurting their ability to recruit and retain top employees.[8]

Time Efficiency

Time pacing refers to creating new products or services, launching new businesses, or entering new markets according to the calendar. Even though time-paced companies can be extraordinarily fast, it is important not to confuse time pacing with speed. By definition, time pacing is regular, rhythmic, and proactive. Time pacing creates a relentless sense of urgency around meeting deadlines and concentrates individual and team energy around common goals. Although the tempo may be fast, it is predictable and thus gives people a sense of control in otherwise chaotic markets. People become focused, efficient, and confident about the task at hand, which leads to enhanced performance.

In addition to creating a sense of urgency, time pacing disciplines managers to excel at two critical, but often neglected, processes essential to success in changing markets. The first is managing transitions, or the shifts from one activity to the next. The second is managing rhythm, or the pace at which companies change. Companies that march to the rhythm of time pacing build momentum. By setting a regular pace for change, managers avoid becoming locked into old patterns and habits. A survey of fifty major U.S. companies found that practically all put time-based strategy, as the new approach is called, at the top of their priority lists because it provides a meaningful competitive advantage.[9]

Managers in complex businesses are gaining a competitive advantage by making radical changes in how they manage time within their companies (see Figures 3.2 through 3.6). These firms can then make faster decisions, develop new products sooner, and respond to their customers' needs quicker than their competition. As a result, they can provide unique value in the markets they service, which can translate to rapid growth and greater profits.[10]

Quickly developing and distributing products or services brings important, competitive benefits. Market share grows because customers love getting their orders fast. Inventories of finished goods shrink because they are not necessary to ensure quick delivery, since the fastest manufacturers can make and ship an order the day it is received. For this reason, costs fall. Many employees become more satisfied because they are working for a more responsive, more successful company and because speeding operations requires giving them more flexibility and responsibility.[11]

FIGURE 3.2. Do I Know How Much Time I Allot to Each Type of Task?

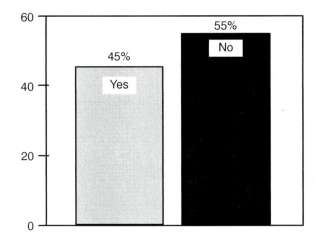

Source: Carter Reengineering Survey (1998).

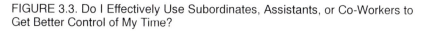

FIGURE 3.3. Do I Effectively Use Subordinates, Assistants, or Co-Workers to Get Better Control of My Time?

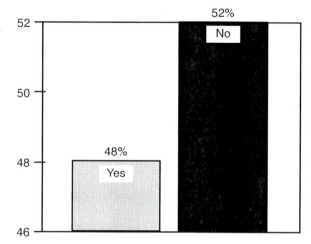

Source: Carter Reengineering Survey (1998).

FIGURE 3.4. Do I Analyze Situations for Time Conservation Possibilities?

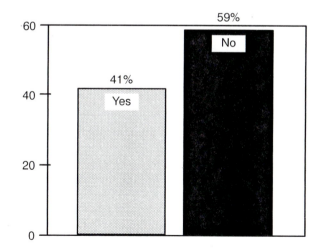

Source: Carter Reengineering Survey (1998).

FIGURE 3.5. Am I Really in Control of My Time? Do I Determine My Activities?

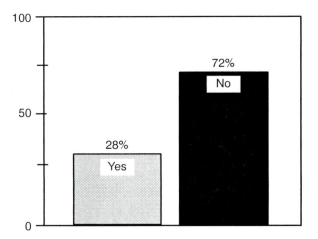

Source: Carter Reengineering Survey (1998).

FIGURE 3.6. Do I Make a Daily Measurement of My Personal Effectiveness?

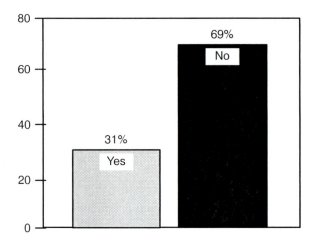

Source: Carter Reengineering Survey (1998).

As a strategic weapon, time is the equivalent of money, productivity, quality, even innovation. Although time is a basic business performance variable, management seldom monitors its consumption explicitly—almost never with the same precision accorded sales and costs. Yet time is a more critical competitive yardstick than traditional financial measurements because of its abstract and finite nature.[12]

Conflict can also be operationalized in terms of time pressure (i.e., the amount of *time remaining* before one must make a decision). There is an interesting relationship between time remaining and selective exposure to information. Under circumstances of high or low time-pressure conflict, people were more likely to request information about a single alternative. Exposure to two alternatives was more likely under moderate levels of time-conflict pressures. Urgency is one form of time pressure. It has been hypothesized that the greater the perceived urgency, the less time devoted to information acquisition.[13]

With cuts in price come lower profit margins. That points to the downside of price cutting, though cuts can spur a quick growth in sales—which are needed in competitive industries. Getting a company into the buying process of potential clients at just the right time can get vital information to the field salespeople when they need it most.

Levi Strauss & Company

Levi Strauss & Company announced to its workers that it was closing the Knoxville factory and ten others in the United States, laying off more than 6,000 employees, or one-third of its domestic workforce. In 1992, the company directed its U.S. plants to abandon the old piecework system, under which a worker repeatedly performed a single, specialized task (such as sewing zippers or attaching belt loops) and was paid according to the amount of work he or she completed. In the new system, groups of ten to thirty-five workers would share the tasks and would be paid according to the total number of trousers the group completed. Levi's figured that this would cut down on the monotony of the old system and enable stitchers to do different tasks, thus reducing repetitive-stress injuries.

At the time, the team concept was a much-touted movement designed to empower factory workers in many industries. Faced with low-cost competitors manufacturing overseas, the San Francisco-based company didn't feel it could keep as many of its U.S. plants open unless it could raise productivity and reduce costs, particularly those incurred by injured workers pushing to make piecework goals. Teamwork, Levi's believed, would be more humane, safe, and profitable. Instead, it led to a quagmire in which skilled workers found themselves pitted against slower colleagues, damaging morale and triggering corrosive infighting, according to more than three dozen employees and managers from several Levi's plants. Longtime friendships dissolved as faster workers tried to banish slower ones.

Teams staffed with skilled equals did fairly well under the new system, and Levi's says it has arranged quotas so the average wage of its manufacturing workforce is higher than it was under the piecework system.

Yet many top performers say the first thing they noticed about teams was that whenever a team member was absent, inexperienced, or just slow, the rest of the team had to make up for it. That infuriated some team members who felt they were carrying subpar workers. With limited supervision from coaches, groups were forced to resolve most work flow and personality issues themselves.

The switch to teams did achieve some of Levi's objectives. Average turnaround, which is the time from when an order is received to when the products are shipped to retail customers, improved from nine to seven weeks. Every sewing team produced bundles of finished pairs of pants every day, so, unlike under the piecework system, there was not as much work in progress. Yet the time saved under teams was often lost en route to retailers. Loaded trucks sometimes sat for weeks outside warehouses, in part because of problems installing new computers and handling facilities, according to former operations managers.

Former managers and Levi's consultants say executives hindered the transition by giving insufficient guidance to supervisors on how to implement the system. As a result, some managers devised their own concepts of teams, improvising everything from pay formulas to shop floor layouts. Employee preparations consisted of brief team-building and problem-solving seminars. At some plants, workers received a book titled *Aftershock: Helping People Through Corporate Change*, including such tips as avoiding negative self-talk and drawing a chart of one's emotional response to change. Workers were allotted time to master unfamiliar machines, but many felt they had inadequate training on issues such as balancing work flows or spotting quality lapses.[14]

EMPLOYEE PERFORMANCE

Research strongly suggests that bosses, albeit accidentally and usually with the best intentions, are often complicit in an employee's lack of success. Research also shows that executives typically compare weaker performers with stronger performers using the following descriptors:

- Less motivated, less energetic, and less likely to go beyond the call of duty
- More passive when it comes to taking charge of problems or projects
- Less aggressive about anticipating problems
- Less innovative and less likely to suggest ideas
- More parochial in their vision and strategic perspective
- More prone to hoard information and assert their authority, making them poor bosses to their own subordinates

It is not surprising that on the basis of these assumptions, managers tend to treat weaker and stronger performers very differently. Indeed, numerous studies have shown that up to 90 percent of all managers treat some subordinates as though they were members of an in-group, while consigning others to membership in an out-group. Members of the in-group are considered the trusted collaborators and therefore receive more autonomy, feedback, and expressions of confidence from their bosses. The boss-subordinate relationship for this group is one of mutual trust and reciprocal influence. Members of the out-group, on the other hand, are regarded more as hired hands and are managed in a more formal, less personal way, with more emphasis on rules, policies, and authority.

The downside of categorical thinking is that in organizations, it ends up hurting subordinates' performance by undermining their motivation in two ways: first, by depriving subordinates of autonomy on the job and, second, by making them feel undervalued. Primarily, poor motivation and assuming subordinates' limited ability means disconnecting them intellectually and emotionally. Tired of being overruled, subordinates simply stop giving their best; and they lose the will to fight for their ideas.

Organizations suffer from the syndrome in several ways. First, uneasy relationships with perceived low performers often drain a manager's emotional and physical energy. It can be quite a strain to keep up a façade of courtesy and pretend everything is fine when both parties know it is not. In addition, the energy devoted to trying to fix these relationships or improve the subordinate's performance through increased supervision prevents the boss from attending to other activities, which often frustrates or even angers the boss. This syndrome can take its toll on a manager's reputation, as other employees in the organization observe his or her behavior toward weaker performers, which may be considered unfair or unsupportive.[15]

> For what is time? Who is able easily and briefly to explain it? . . . . Surely we understand it well enough when we speak of it . . . . What then is time? If nobody asks me, I know; but if I were desirous to explain it to someone . . . plainly, I know not.
>
> St. Augustine

CASE STUDY

Moore University Hospital

Calvin Sprung was recently asked to take on the responsibility of forty-four more staff with another unit in the hospital. Calvin has firsthand experience with Urgency Theory. He finds it is the same as being asked to have increased workload with half the time to accomplish anything. Calvin works on urgency theory almost every day, and he has been reorganizing his own way of managing by restructuring his staff. Specific staff members have their own job titles and responsibilities, and Calvin has delegated most of the day-to-day paperwork to each of these individuals, while giving them a time frame in which to get this work done. One staff member is responsible for the daily traffic control of the unit. Another is responsible for the monthly scheduling of all employees. All of this is unit specific.

Currently, the hospital facility that Calvin is affiliated with has implemented a safety committee structure that takes a minimum of two months to cycle information through. The facility's Environment of Care council (parent safety council) and its subsafety affiliate councils meet bimonthly to discuss relevant issues and regulatory requirements that are within the responsibility of the council and its leaders. The structure is designed such that the subsafety councils are charged with the assessment, discussion, and resolution of safety and environment of care (e.g., safety, industrial hygiene, fire safety, utility safety, disaster preparedness, hazardous materials, and medical equipment). Issues include routine requirements, sentinel events, and quality assessment/improvement. The subsafety council chairperson then reports, during the following month, the issues discussed and their respective status and outcomes to the parent safety council. Again, this is for the purpose of seeking direction, assistance, and/or approval. The parent council, required by health care regulations, reports to a senior leadership council that reports to the board of governors. This is how the management of information is conducted with regard to the facility's safety program.

Do you have any suggestions for Calvin concerning the conditions he faces that can minimize urgency theory's problems and enhance its advantages?

Chapter 4

Customer Focus

INTRODUCTION

Senior executives need to make market focus a personal, strategic priority to initiate organizational change. Most top-level managers routinely spend time visiting customers, but frequently, these visits are superficial, and the managers do not invest the effort needed to understand and empathize with the customer. Top-level managers need to spend a day in the life of key customers in their business processes. There is no substitute for managers' instincts, imagination, and personal knowledge of the market.[1] Treating customers and shareholders with honesty and respect is a good start, if a company really wants to improve service.[2] Companies depend on customers for their existence, but businesses are often organized for their own convenience rather than the customer's. Self-directed teams, however, help make a company truly customer focused.[3]

Reengineering is something that should be used primarily for major processes that play a significant role, such as customer service or sales activity. Effective reengineering looks at doing things most effectively and asks the following questions: What are our core competencies? Where should we compete? What is our distinctive advantage? How do our customers define value? What changes should we make to adjust to changes in the marketplace?

The key focus with reengineering is to work on the process. There is the threat of bringing in changes and even possible job losses, and the necessity of changing due to competitive and marketplace forces can dictate the need for urgent changes. Then positioning to face these challenges in the form of good leadership, enhanced skills, and team involvement becomes necessary. The

55

result, if successful, is achievement and empowerment. The strategic approach to reengineering involves defining goals and the business process, listening to customers, benchmarking, using tools such as technology, where appropriate, developing a reengineering plan of action, and monitoring and evaluating outcomes.

CUSTOMERS AND REENGINEERING

Managers can play an essential role during reengineering by bringing the customer into the process (see Figure 4.1). Radical changes in the business environment have dictated the need for reengineering in organizations. These changes in the marketplace have involved developments such as technology, sophisticated customers, globalization, company mergers and acquisitions, rising business and sales costs, impact of the quality movement, communication volume and speed, and the need for adaptable, flexible,

FIGURE 4.1. Key: Bring the Customer into the Process and Develop a Builder Mentality

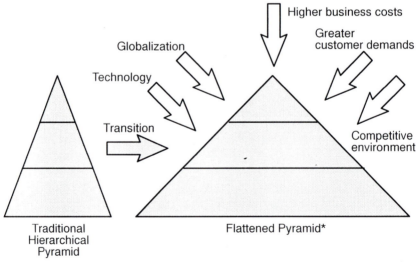

* Marketplace changes have forced organizations to reengineer and create the "flattened pyramid."

agile organizations. The manager's importance to the reengineering process can be to remind the organization that radical process innovation should consider marketplace perspectives and not just the internal perspectives of senior-level management and the company.

Reengineering can bring dramatic process improvements that are too often only demonstrated in individual process areas, not in sales revenue results. Managers can play a key role in companywide reengineering. In addition to giving employees and salespeople convincing reasons for a new design and the ability to provide feedback in the form of concerns and suggestions, management must also look outside the organization to the customers for direction.[4] The drive to win more business from those ever-smarter customers has spurred a wave of change in the sales profession. Many leading companies are completely overhauling the way they hire, organize, train, and compensate their sales forces. Their aim is to turn their salespeople into smart *businesspeople.*

Managers generally view reengineering as change that occurs quickly and dramatically and involves the radical redesign of cross-functional business processes. A study of reengineering projects at forty companies during the last three years observed several instances in which senior executives slowed down the pace of change and modified ambitious reengineering goals. Although these companies did not gain the breakthrough improvements often promised by proponents of radical reengineering, they nonetheless reduced the cost of specific processes by 30 to 50 percent, shortened cycle times, and dramatically improved service to their customers.[5]

To stay ahead of the competition some companies are hiring representatives who are industry experts, not mere glad-handing extroverts. They are also organizing their sales forces around customer industries and national accounts, not just geographic territories. In addition, companies train salespeople to probe customers' business problems, not peddle products and manipulate buyers. They are compensating salespeople for building long-term partnerships with customers, not for driving short-term revenues. Sales forces are expected to deal with complex issues and problems, and they're expected to come in and size up the situation. Reengineering the organization around customers and channels is one of the major ways sales forces are starting to achieve significant revenue gains and cost reductions.[6]

Effective marketing relies on a two-way information flow between the marketer and the prospect. Marketers must collect detailed demographic and lifestyle information about large numbers of consumers to determine effective market segments. Then they must integrate this mass of information into a concrete understanding of what products different consumers want and what they are willing to pay.[7] Fundamental reengineering means adopting a new marketing approach. The most common one observed is mass customization. Rather than mass-market a standard service to all customers, mass customization produces and delivers individualized services to each customer and at costs competitive with mass production.

Value Focus

Firms are focusing on what adds value for the customer and eliminating what does not. This means that firms have to ask themselves "Is what we're doing useful enough for someone to pay money for it?" Although value means different things to different people, it consists of intrinsic product features, service, and price, but price is not everything in determining value. For example, a study by Grey Advertising determined that only 37 percent of its customers currently compared prices, contrasted with 54 percent in 1991.[8]

With deregulation and a growing global economy, service marketers now face pressures experienced by product companies a decade ago. The new value concept offers *individualized* benefits rather than more standardized offerings. Thus, the strategy of producing more of the same service is replaced by innovation and differentiation based on mass customization. Since sophisticated services such as finance or insurance are knowledge based and information intensive, the marketing goal is to reengineer them to integrate knowledge and information in a way that is different and better than the competition. Reengineering is about business reinvention—not business improvement, business enhancement, or business modification. Reengineering should only be done when a need exists for a major overhaul.

A business insurance seller reengineered its organization so that agents could do complete policy illustrations and ready-to-sign contracts in the field with customers. Previously, headquarters staff controlled the data necessary to complete a policy and were perceived by agents as unnecessary middlemen who slowed or sometimes killed the sale. The new approach is agent focused, not only by giving each agent a personal computer, but also by transferring systems and data processing staff into the field closer to the point of sale. Agents can tap the necessary data from across the corporation, perform needs analysis instantly as the customer looks on, and illustrate various insurance programs to satisfy specific customer requirements. The internal support structure that makes this possible is invisible to customers, who view the buying process as seamless and not entangled in insurance company bureaucracy.

Evidence suggests that corporate reengineering may trigger the outsourcing of an internal activity to an external supplier. The objective is to free up company technology, systems, and staff for more strategic activities. For example, Eastman Kodak turned over the management and maintenance of its telecommunications system to Digital Equipment Corporation to concentrate on imaging technology. Xerox Corporation also outsourced many computing activities as part of its back-office reengineering. The resulting services contract with Electronic Data Systems (EDS), estimated at $4 billion, makes it one of the largest outsourcing deals in history.

Value-Added Features

A *process* is a collection of activities that takes one or more kinds of input and creates an output that is of value to the customer. Service marketers are reengineering customer engagement approaches to find opportunities that create new market segments rather than share existing ones with competition. Reengineering projects have been initiated to search for prospects in areas never before considered. Reengineering has proven an effective way to cut costs and reduce payrolls. However, reengineering gets just as much impact from increasing sales as it does from decreasing costs, either by taking market share from competitors or generating new products and services.[9]

The value-added feature is not in the product anymore; it is in the relationship between the company and its customers. In an economy with euphemistic concepts such as downsizing and reengineering, there had to be added value in giving customers the help companies no longer had in house. If customers perceive a high level of expertise, and it can help them, companies are worth more to them.[10]

Too many managers feel the only time they need to restructure their departments or sales force is after something major has happened, such as losing a big account. Many do not think ahead and realize that a realignment may be able to help problems that have not even come up yet. The best companies first focus on which customers they want to serve and then learn what those customers want and how they can fulfill those needs (see Figure 4.2 for an example of how to evaluate the need to reengineer).

Studies show that 80 percent of the companies in the United States have imbalanced alignments. They have too many salespeople in one territory and too few in another. This is costing companies 2 to 7 percent in sales losses every year. Realignment is not a static concept that only happens once during the life cycle of a company. Usually, it is an evolutionary process that is implemented in various stages to meet new customer or industry demands. Competitive firms are always aware of the chance for change. They are the ones that are always surveying their customers and sales representatives to find out what they want. They are also keeping a keen eye on the competition and staying aware of the changing nature of their marketplace. Then, they are acting upon these changes and needs.

The only way American companies can survive today is by moving from an internally based product focus to a more external customer focus. Sales forces that take the time to understand their customers and learn what they want are the ones that will succeed. The most important thing is understanding and meeting the needs of the customer.[11] Figure 4.2 shows an example of a value-added process used to monitor and track customer transactions.

Customer Satisfaction

Hundreds of Fortune 500 companies and many small and midsize companies have some sort of customer satisfaction initiative under way. Such companies as Dow Chemical, Eastman Chemical, IBM, Ralston Purina, 3M, and Xerox are surveying customers and collecting data on satisfaction levels. The reasons are to identify and resolve obstacles for better customer relations, to formulate sales and marketing strategies, and to retool sales and service skills.

FIGURE 4.2. Evaluate the Existing Process to Determine the Need to Reengineer

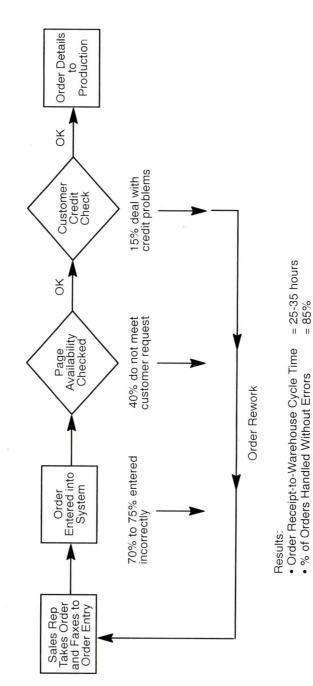

Results:
- Order Receipt-to-Warehouse Cycle Time = 25-35 hours
- % of Orders Handled Without Errors = 85%
- Cost Per Order As a % of Revenues = 16%

Too often, customer satisfaction initiatives fail, or provide misleading results, because they ask the wrong questions of the wrong people and produce data that are used in the wrong way. The problem is compounded when companies fail to inform the customers they have surveyed of how their input has changed the way the company does business. On the other hand, the companies that have successfully used customer surveys have learned key lessons: how customer satisfaction is measured can often be as important as what is measured, and having an adaptable surveying methodology ensures that listening to the voice of the customer is being market driven.

For example, Xerox uses phone surveys and goes after decision makers exclusively, conducting about 10,000 surveys per month. It has also gone beyond measuring customer satisfaction to gauging customer loyalty as well. Xerox continues to measure satisfaction, but also asks whether the customer would recommend Xerox to an associate and whether he or she would buy from Xerox again. The company also tracks survey data by three classes of customer—first-time buyers, replacement or upgrade buyers, and additional buyers—giving the company a finer read on who purchases what, when, and why.

Xerox has also implemented a Customer Relationship Assessment survey for its top customers. The goal, again, is to go beyond satisfaction to look at customer loyalty. These are face-to-face surveys conducted by the account management teams of about 500 global, national, or "named" accounts that are essentially Xerox's best customers.[12]

Businesses have been trying to become more profitable by reengineering and downsizing. Winning more business from existing customers is critical to meeting that objective. IBM underwent a major sales force reorganization when Louis Gerstner took over as chairman. A major reason why Big Blue was floundering at the time was that salespeople had lost touch with customers and had failed to spot new revenue opportunities. Droves of sellers representing multiple fiefdoms of IBM—hardware, software, consulting services—would call on a client, only creating confusion. Many customers, particularly major ones, wanted a single face that represented IBM's vast array of products and services.

Consequently, one of Gerstner's first moves was to implement a system in which a single client executive would work with accounts and manage teams of product representatives, systems engineers, and consultants within IBM. Those client executives have become, in effect, experts in the customers' industries.

The term *partnering* gets bandied about in business circles. For companies that are building lasting relationships with clients, the concept is simple—partnering means becoming part of the customer's business fabric. Partnering also means continually finding ways to provide more value to customers by jointly developing new products to help them improve their business processes. The goal is to become so enmeshed with customers that they naturally come to that particular firm for solutions, and the salespeople become virtual employees of the customers' company. Being a consultant with customers also often means educating them about the full range of a company's products. [13]

Customer Focus

Customer orientation is making the greatest inroads in the business world. In a recent Forum Corporation survey, more than 600 executives were asked, "What are your organization's most important strategic needs?" Of the respondents, 86 percent answered "quality of customer service." Unfortunately, although many organizations make a serious effort to find out what their customers want, they do not effectively use this potentially powerful data.

By failing to follow up, these companies deny themselves a great opportunity. Today, being customer focused is not enough. When management incorporates the voice of the customer into the company, and then acts on it, the organization is transformed. It goes from being merely customer focused to being customer driven. In the era of the customer, the companies that succeed will be the ones who reshape the "interesting" data from their customer research and drive it through their organizations in imaginative and powerful ways. [14]

As communication tools become interactive, managers talk more about goals that pertain to individual relationships, such as share of customer requirements, customer contact outcomes, and customer satisfaction measures. Managers have begun to think of good marketing as good conversation and as a process of drawing potential customers into progressively more satisfying back-and-forth relationships with the company. American Airlines' use of the frequent flier program in 1981 triggered other industries to create membership clubs. Retention programs, if skillfully designed, can be much more than volume discount programs. They can inspire loyalty from the market's biggest spenders. The key is to deliver benefits that appeal more to heavy users than to light users, draw attention to a brand's claimed distinction, and enliven the buying experience so that the heavy user becomes an even heavier user.[15]

For example, resellers of long distance telephone service have gained market share at the expense of the major carriers in the United States, while in Europe, travel agents undercut the airlines by buying blocks of seats from whoever has the lowest rates at any given time and then reselling them. However, interconnection also allows competitors to become a source of customers for one another when one provider originates traffic and another eventually delivers it.

Networks

Network-based businesses are those which deliver a significant portion of their value to their customers by transporting people, goods, or information from any entry point on a network to any exit point. These businesses can be categorized by the degree to which their value to customers resides in the network or in the individual outlets.[16]

Most industries are struggling under worldwide overcapacity; steadily improving productivity maintains this glut even as companies shut down plants. The Atlanta-based unit of Siemens that makes heavy electrical equipment and motors has halved floor space since 1986, yet is producing 50 percent more. Buyers are in just the mood to push such companies to the wall.[17]

Ninety percent of accounts leave because they feel badly treated and unappreciated. That should serve as a warning signal to companies to make sure their perception of customer satisfaction matches the reality. Implementing a process to repair its damaged accounts by identifying the problems, meeting with the customer and assessing the damage, and focusing time and attention on fixing the situation is part of the recovery.

Management should devise a realistic strategy to repair the client relationship. Once a reconciliation with a customer is reached, companies should notify everyone involved. "Organized learning must take place, not just in marketing and sales departments, but companywide. Share the story with everyone in the organization so it does not happen again."[18] Customer focus should always be a top priority during, and after, any reengineering effort.

CASE STUDY

Reinglass Bank

Synopsis of Issue

The challenge is to achieve optimum "face time" with clients to maximize business opportunities, while attending to all of the other necessary activities in support of the sales process.

Background

Reinglass Bank is responsible for generating annuity revenue by selling a variety of payment-related service products to large corporate clients of the bank. These products encompass checks, wires, and electronic payment vehicles; investment products; and balance and transaction reporting. These services are provided by Reinglass Bank on a global basis.

Description of Issue

One of the biggest management challenges Laura Marsiello faces, as does her entire sales organization that she manages, is achieving the optimal level of face time with clients. Face time means engaging the client in meaningful discussions, primarily in person, that lead to needs assessment and, ultimately, solutions.

The two key factors in determining a successful face time process are:

1. achieving an effective proactive calling program with each major client, and
2. effectively managing a variety of other activities, including administration, management information systems (MIS), problem solving, research, and other related functions.

The administrative and support functions cover a variety of tasks that can, at times, be extremely time-consuming. A host of reporting needs includes call memos, deal tracking, weekly highlights, and e-mail communication, to mention a few. Laura's sales professionals, although supported by customer service officers, perform a number of customer service functions, particularly when a serious problem or situation arises. There are also a number of internal meetings that sales reps are required to attend, including monthly team meetings, sales communication meetings, and periodic training sessions. Although all these activities and meetings are important to the bank's success, they can consume, in some cases, 60 percent of the sales representatives' time.

The following are some of the solutions that Laura has implemented:

- Reduce the number of internal meetings.
- Streamline the MIS process.
- Provide remote access to internal networks and communication systems.

Although many of these fixes have helped, the problem still exists. We must continue to find ways of increasing our interaction with clients to maximize opportunities for our business.

You are a fellow manager of Laura's with a branch office of Reinglass Bank in another city. Laura now faces the same problem that you have already solved through the necessary changes. What would you advise Laura to do?

·Chapter 5

New Management Tools

INTRODUCTION

Various management tools and concepts have emerged from the use of reengineering to create and maintain improvements in organizations. Reengineering initiatives frequently focus at the process level on only a single function and do not include the entire value chain (suppliers and customers). Improvement projects utilize value analysis on each task, step, and element in a process. Problems are identified, prioritized, and analyzed to assess their root cause, and the process is adjusted accordingly. Since the scope of these improvements tends to be narrow, it usually takes less than one year for implementation.

BUSINESS PROCESS REENGINEERING

Business process reengineering (BPR) or process redesign not only focuses on the process level but also includes the entire value chain. BPR initiatives are output or result driven. Organizations that embrace BPR should first ask whether the output or result is valued by the customer. If the product/output is valued, then new ways to deliver the process are identified, evaluated, and, if feasible, implemented. By starting with a white piece of paper, old, no longer valid paradigms are left by the wayside and breakthrough improvements occur.

All organizations, regardless of size or sophistication, are structured around three elements: technology, organization, and processes. Technology consists of that used to transform inputs into outputs, or data, which is the information used to make business decisions and applications (e.g., software). In addition, the organization includes the organization's structure, the way jobs are designed, human resources systems, workforce competencies, administrative control systems, and culture. Last, the process consists of the work processes and the physical layout of an organization's architecture. Managing the integration of each of these elements makes BPR and business reengineering difficult and risky to implement successfully. Conversely, process improvement initiatives usually focus on only the process element of architecture.

BUSINESS REENGINEERING

Business reengineering focuses on the enterprise level of an organization. This type of reengineering is unlike BPR because it focuses primarily on the strategic aspects of an organization. Business reengineering tends to be vision driven and answers such fundamental questions as the following: Are we in the right business? Who are our customers? On a macro level, what products and services should we be delivering?

Reengineering's Effectiveness

One leading consulting firm's 1994 study found that 62 percent of surveyed executives whose companies are currently undertaking reengineering initiatives reported that their reengineering initiatives have achieved most of their desired goals (see Figure 5.1). In another study conducted by a prominent accounting firm, 61 percent of chief financial officers (CFOs) surveyed reported that reengineering produced "tenfold improvement," "met all initial goals," or "provided a positive experience."

The extent to which reengineering has been successful should be viewed as a function of several criteria, such as realistic management expectations, performance measures, and scope. Viewing a reengineering initiative through those perspectives provides a more accurate assessment of progress. According to a leading consulting firm's study of companies that had implemented reengineering, the major-

FIGURE 5.1. Percentage of Managers Who Felt Their Organizations Were Made Better by Reengineering

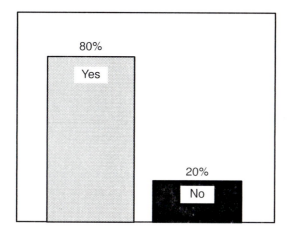

Source: Carter Reengineering Survey (1998).

ity of respondents targeted cost reductions (69 percent), productivity increase (53 percent), and cycle-time reductions (49 percent) as their primary performance measures. Quality improvement proved to be the easiest target to meet (69 percent), reflecting the more tactical nature of such goals. Cost reduction (55 percent), productivity increase (50 percent), and cycle-time reduction (48 percent) were the next easiest to meet. Customer satisfaction improvement (44 percent), which spans both tactical and strategic realms, was difficult to achieve. Not surprisingly, strategic targets such as increasing revenue (46 percent) and market share (38 percent) represented the most difficult types of results to realize.

To successfully achieve the desired goals from their reengineering initiatives, companies must carefully choose and manage the business areas that will best yield the desired results. According to one leading reengineering study of North American businesses, 25 percent of respondents chose customer service manufacturing/production (15 percent), sales and marketing (11 percent), procurement (9 percent), information systems (6 percent), distribution (4 percent), and product development (4 percent).[1]

BALANCED SCORECARD

As managers and academic researchers have tried to remedy the inadequacies of current performance measurement systems, some have focused on making financial measures more relevant. Senior executives realize that no single measure can provide a clear performance target or focus attention on critical areas of the business. Managers want a balanced presentation of both financial and operational measures.

The balanced scorecard includes financial measures that tell the results of actions already taken. It complements the financial measures with operational measures on customer satisfaction, internal processes, and the organization's innovation and improvement activities—measures that are the drivers of future financial performance.

The balanced scorecard allows managers to look at the business from four important perspectives, providing answers to four basic questions:

1. How do customers see us? (customer perspective)
2. What must we excel at? (internal perspective)
3. Can we continue to improve and create value? (innovation and learning perspective)
4. How do we look to shareholders? (financial perspective)

The balanced scorecard forces managers to focus on the handful of measures that are most critical.

1. Initially developed as an enhanced measurement system, the balanced scorecard is, in fact, a management system that can motivate breakthrough performance.
2. The scorecard translates a business unit's mission and strategy into a set of measures built around the following four perspectives:

   • Financial—"How do we look to our shareholders?"
   • Customer—"How do we become our customers' most valued supplier?"

- Internal Processes—"What processes—both long term and short term—must we excel at to achieve our financial and customer objectives?"
- Innovation and Improvement—"How can we continue to improve and create value, particularly in regard to employee capabilities and motivation and the rate of improvement of existing processes?"

How a company is performing from its customers' perspective has become, therefore, a priority for top management. The balanced scorecard demands that managers translate their general mission statement on customer service into specific measures that reflect the factors that really matter to customers.

Customer-based measures are important, but they must be translated into measures of what the company must do internally to meet its customers' expectations. Managers need to focus on those critical internal operations which enable them to satisfy customer needs. The second part of the balanced scorecard gives managers that internal perspective.

The internal measures for the balanced scorecard should stem from the business processes that have the greatest impact on customer satisfaction—factors that affect cycle time, quality, employee skills, and productivity, for example. Companies should also attempt to identify and measure their company's core competencies, the critical technologies needed to ensure continued market leadership. Companies should decide what processes and competencies they must excel at and specify measures for each.

A company's ability to innovate, improve, and learn is tied directly to the company's value. That is, only through the ability to launch new products, create more value for customers, and improve operating efficiencies continually can a company penetrate new markets and increase revenues and margins—in short, grow, and thereby increase shareholder value.

Financial performance measures indicate whether the company's strategy, implementation, and execution are contributing to bottom-line improvement. Typical financial goals relate to profitability, growth, and shareholder value. A failure to convert improved operational performance, as measured in the scorecard, into improved financial performance should send executives back to their drawing boards to rethink the company's strategy or its implementation plans.

The balanced scorecard is well-suited to the kind of organization many companies are trying to become.

- It makes strategy operational by translating strategy into performance measures and targets.
- It helps focus the entire organization on what must be done to create breakthrough performance.
- It can act as an integrating device, an umbrella, for a variety of diverse, often disconnected, corporate programs, such as quality, reengineering, process redesign, and customer service.
- Corporate-level measures can be broken down to lower levels in the organization so that local managers, operators, and employees can see what they must do well to improve organizational effectiveness.
- It provides a comprehensive view that overturns the traditional idea of the organization as a collection of isolated, independent functions and departments.

The scorecard puts strategy and vision, not control, at the center. It establishes goals but assumes that people will adopt whatever behaviors and take whatever actions are necessary to arrive at those goals. The measures are designed to pull people toward the overall vision. Senior managers may know what the end result should be, but they cannot tell employees exactly how to achieve that result, if only because the conditions in which employees operate are constantly changing.

This new approach to performance measurement is consistent with the initiatives under way in many companies: cross-functional integration, customer-supplier partnerships, global scale, continuous improvement, and team rather than individual accountability. By combining the financial, customer, internal process and innovation, and organizational learning perspectives, the balanced scorecard helps managers understand, at least implicitly, many interrelationships.[2]

Many companies that are now attempting to implement local improvement programs such as process reengineering and employee empowerment lack a sense of integration. The balanced scorecard can serve as the focal point for the organization's efforts, defining and communicating priorities to managers, employees, investors, and even customers. The balanced scorecard is not a template that can be applied to businesses in general or even industrywide. Different market situations, product strategies, and competitive environments require different scorecards. Business units devise customized scorecards to fit their mission, strategy, technology, and culture.[3]

As companies around the world adapt themselves for competition that is based on information, their ability to exploit intangible assets has become far more decisive than their ability to invest in and manage physical assets. Creating a scorecard takes longer, but it offers several advantages: information from a larger number of managers is incorporated into the internal objectives, the managers gain a better understanding of the company's long-term strategic goals, and such broad participation builds a stronger commitment to achieving those goals.

The balanced scorecard shows what the organization is trying to achieve for shareholders and customers alike. Balanced scorecard users generally engage in three activities: communicating and educating, setting goals, and linking rewards to performance measures.

Building a balanced scorecard also creates a framework for managing an organization's various change programs. These initiatives, such as reengineering, employee empowerment, and time-based management, promise to deliver results but also compete with one another for scarce resources, including the scarcest resource of all—senior managers' time and attention.

Why Companies Need a Balanced Scorecard

- No single measure or set of measures can adequately guide and motivate the current actions that will drive future performance.
- Financial results report past performance but are not adequate predictors or drivers of future performance. Even current financial performance may be distorted by omitting the effects of current actions that have created or destroyed future value. Companies need to balance short-term financial performance with long-term growth opportunities.

- Companies must link their strategic objectives to a set of financial and operational measures to clarify and communicate the objectives and use them for evaluating performance.

Without a balanced scorecard, most organizations are unable to achieve a similar consistency of vision and action as they attempt to change direction and introduce new strategies and processes. The balanced scorecard provides a framework for managing the implementation of strategy, while also allowing the strategy itself to evolve in response to changes in the company's competitive, market, and technological environments.[4]

The balanced scorecard may seem to many managers to be "much ado about nothing," since measuring performance and assessing areas for improvement in organizations is nothing new. However, the balanced scorecard employs a framework with four precise performance criteria—innovation, financial perspectives, customer perspectives, and internal perspectives—that make its application manageable, thorough, and easy to administer.

VIRTUAL OFFICES

There are different ways to use technology to stay in front of clients. Some are simple, such as a weekly audioconference during which representatives dial in and ask questions or broadcast a message over voice mail to the entire sales force and ask for replies to be sent to a specific voice mailbox. Other ways to virtually reach out to a team could include an interactive quiz delivered via a multimedia application.[5]

Eventually, many different models for building virtual factories are likely to arise. They may be starlike structures with dominant centers or manufacturing communities in which groups of small manufacturers band together for the same kinds of benefits available to large traditional factories with abundant resources for expanding information technology. The rigid formulation of traditional electronic data interchange will give way to a world of greater fluidity. Once the benefits of the real virtual office have been demonstrated, they will create a new business world.[6]

For a team to work effectively, its members need to trust one another. They need to be sure that everyone will fulfill his or her obligations and behave in a consistent, predictable manner. Trust can and does exist in virtual teams, but it develops in a very different way than in traditional teams. Past studies of teams have shown that trust tends to evolve in three stages. First comes deterrence-based trust: team members do what they say they will do simply because they fear they will be punished if they do not. Then, as members become more and more familiar with one another, knowledge-based trust develops: each member knows his or her teammates well enough to predict their behavior with confidence. Finally, identification-based trust emerges: trust is built on empathy and shared values; members are able to put themselves in their teammates' place.

What drives the evolution of trust in conventional settings is direct, face-to-face interaction, the kind of interaction that does not take place in virtual teams. Trust in virtual teams tends to be established, or not, right at the outset. The first interactions of the team members are crucial. Teams with the highest levels of trust tended to share three traits. First, they began their interactions with a series of social messages—introducing themselves and providing some personal background—before focusing on the work at hand. Second, they set clear roles for each team member. Assigning each member a particular task enabled all of them to identify with one another, forging a foundation for identification-based trust. The third hallmark of the trusting team had to do with attitude: team members consistently displayed eagerness, enthusiasm, and an intense action orientation in all their messages. One pessimist has the potential to undermine an entire virtual team.[7]

Today's technology has telescoped product and process life cycles so much that skills are becoming obsolete at a breathtaking pace. Instead of paying for a job, employers are now paying for a variety of skills that workers acquire. Many manufacturers have found that teams of cross-trained workers are vital to quality improvement. They can detect flaws in one another's work, apply problem-solving techniques more effectively, and fill in for one another as needed—critical in just-in-time systems that function without mountainous buffers of inventory and work in progress.

At the same time, giving workers more skills and autonomy can confuse middle managers stripped of traditional responsibilities and thrust into roles that emphasize counseling and coaching over directing and enforcing. With workers doing their own sourcing, scheduling, and inspection, middle-level managers are no longer as necessary to handle overseeing all of those functions.[8]

Virtual operations come with their own set of management challenges, and managers must be skillful enough to recognize those challenges and rise to them. Managers need to practice the following list to make a virtual operation work:

1. Make sure senior managers operate virtually at least part of the time.
2. Visit remote offices frequently.
3. Make sure that employees have a workspace that promotes productivity.
4. Help remote workers form strong ties to people at the central office.
5. Find ways to compensate for the loss of daily, face-to-face contact.
6. Counteract the sense among remote workers that they're missing out on key business advances.[9]

Banking

Similar to other big banks, Chase is racing to build a computer network of database marketing capability that can mine customer data for sales opportunities. Most Chase customers are either credit card users or customers of its regional banks. The company hopes a database will sell more products to more people.

Several big banks are gunning for the same customers as Chase—via branches. NationsBank Corporation and BankAmerica Corporation agreed to a merger that will create a behemoth with roughly 4,900 branches from Florida to California. Banc One Corporation and First Chicago NBD Corporation, meanwhile, also announced a merger that will create a Midwest giant. Both newly formed companies will seek to lure customers away from Chase in such areas as student lending, auto lending, and mortgages.[10]

Roughly 4.5 to 5 million people, or about 5 percent of the nation's households, use some form of online banking, up from about 200,000 in early 1995. That figure will balloon to about 22 million, or 21 percent of U.S. households, by the end of 2001. Although banks across the nation are trying to establish a stronger presence on the World Wide Web, pure Internet banks are a nascent sector. Instead of walking into a branch, customers gain access to their accounts through personal computers. They can make deposits, transfer funds, pay bills, and apply for loans twenty-four hours a day, seven days a week.[11]

OUTSOURCING

About one-third of Fortune 1000 industrial corporations out-source more than 50 percent of their manufacturing capacity. This work outsourced by these firms totaled about $200 billion a year.[12]

While the principal objective of some corporations has been to maintain or even maximize its employment levels, others have found that the threat of the lack of profits dictates cutting back employment to only the number needed to operate efficiently. Outsourcing has become one of the creative alternatives to downsizing because it helps firms to realize cost savings and productivity increases, despite staff cuts that they have made.[13]

There are compelling business reasons for companies to hand over more of their nonstrategic activities to an outside provider. The number of new outsourcing service providers is escalating, and established providers are expanding their offerings.[14]

Downsizing and outsourcing are opening tremendous opportunities for small companies. The secret to making a deal is twofold. First, determine what a big company needs to increase sales or improve customer service; second, find the person to whom to make a pitch. Large companies have realized that the world has changed and that many innovations are coming out of small companies.

The core competence concept helps top managers answer the fundamental question "What should we do?" The business processes perspective addresses the question "How should we do it?" Some activities are performed so much better than the competition and are so critical to end products or services that they can be described as core competencies. When a series of activities are organized into a system that works better than the sum of its parts, this business process can also create competitive advantage, even if component activities by themselves do not.

Outsourcing involves contracting out significant support activities that would be prohibitively expensive or even impossible to duplicate internally. By identifying the firm's own resources based on a set of core competencies, a company can distinguish itself from competitors and provide value to customers. Outsourcing noncore competencies can decrease risk, shorten cycle times, lower costs, and create better responsiveness to customer needs.

In the process of outsourcing, it is important to do the following:

- *Evaluate costs.* Try to determine just how much is being spent on a function and whether or not it can be done more cheaply by an outside company.
- *Set objectives.* Realistically decide what an outsource partner can do for the company. Whether it is to cut costs, improve focus, or free up resources, make certain the goals are attainable.
- *Be cautious.* Do not select an outsource partner without careful examination.
- *Monitor.* If you decide to outsource, set up regular performance reviews or similar criteria to measure the provider's performance. Outsourcing isn't an excuse to overlook an aspect of your business.
- *Be flexible.* Even after deciding to outsource, look at ways it can be improved. Do not be afraid to make changes in the ways a process is being handled.
- *Avoid jumping on the bandwagon.* Just because outsourcing is a growing trend does not mean it should be automatically embraced. If a change is not needed, do not make one just for the sake of it.[15]

TECHNOLOGY

More than any other agent of change, information technology is transforming the way business works. It is helping companies get leaner, smarter, and closer to the customer. Those who seize the opportunities inherent in this revolution are capturing important competitive advantages.[16]

Reeling from reengineering and downsizing, and facing the rapid progress of information technology, workforces need to know how to ride the computer wave to remain competitive. Today's effective corporations, such as DuPont, Motorola, and GTE, are making computer training a top priority. Understanding the value and benefits of good computer training is important. (See Figure 5.1 for benefits of different technology tools.)

Electronics and mobile communications giant Motorola, for example, spends $140 million a year training employees through Motorola University, its in-house training facility. This "university without walls" consists of fourteen sites worldwide, with the hub at corporate headquarters in Schaumburg, Illinois. Training at Motorola University in standard software programs and applications is offered in a classroom setting. Each of the corporation's business units, which include cellular operations, paging, and semiconductors, also offers its own courses in custom programs specific to that unit.[17]

For the many information users in large organizations, effective information management must begin by thinking about how people use information, not with how people use machines. Few compa-

FIGURE 5.1. Technology Tools

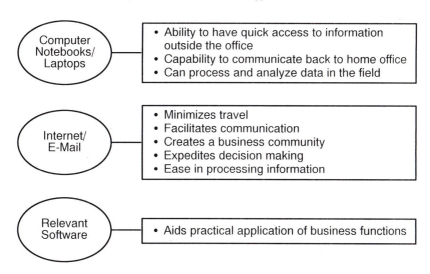

nies have undertaken such planning with any concern for how people actually use information. Most approaches have addressed only a small fraction of organizations' information, which is that found on computers. Yet, evidence from research conducted since the mid-1960s shows that most managers do not rely on computer-based information to make decisions.[18]

The process analysis, reengineering, and streamlining work are done with the emerging technologies and the applications that are out there. If you put the two together and do it reasonably well, then you have a transformation. People are realizing that you cannot change the tools and expect on day one that everyone will embrace new solutions. Only about 10 to 20 percent of companies are willing to reengineer themselves by starting from scratch.[19]

The Internet poses a difficult challenge for established businesses. The Internet lets companies build interactive relationships with customers and suppliers and deliver new products and services at very low cost. Internet commerce is such a new phenomenon, and so much about it is uncertain and confusing, that it is difficult for executives at most companies, new or old, to decide the best way to use this channel. It becomes even more difficult for organizations to accurately estimate the returns on any Internet investment they may make.

Companies can establish a direct link to customers through the Internet to complete transactions or trade information more easily. They can use the Internet to develop and deliver new products and services for new customers, and a company could conceivably use the Internet to become the dominant player in the electronic channel of a specific industry or segment, controlling access to customers and setting new business rules. By exploring the opportunities and threats they face in each of these four domains, executives can realistically assess what, if any, investments they should begin to make in Internet commerce and determine what risks will need to be anticipated. A sound Internet commerce strategy begins by articulating what is possible.

Companies are giving customers just about the same level of service through the Internet that they can currently get directly from a salesperson. Visitors to a company's Web site can hunt for a part by its number, by a description, or by its manufacturer. They can place an order for parts, pay for them electronically, track the status of previous orders, and even speed delivery time by connecting directly from a Web site to the shipping company's site. Companies are also using new Internet technologies to personalize interactions with their customers and build customer loyalty. One way is to tailor the information and options customers see at a site to just what they want.[20]

As with the fax machine and personal computer that preceded it, e-mail is a technological tool that many can scarcely comprehend doing without. E-mail has become a fundamental part of corporate communications. It also flattens corporate hierarchies. Any employee can have instant access to executives with a few strokes of the keyboard. For those sales managers who practically live on the road, e-mail provides an opportunity to be in touch with a team twenty-four hours a day. However, e-mail should never replace face-to-face meetings, either with clients or with employees, on important issues. If the customer expresses some kind of concern about an issue, it's best to get on the phone or make an appointment to see the person. A recent study by UCLA and Arthur Andersen that surveyed 1,500 workers found that the primary use of e-mail is "to chat with other employees." Only 22 percent indicate they use the technology to talk to clients.[21]

Videoconferencing seems easy, since by using the latest in technology, executives can conduct interactive meetings. By far, the most important step in successful videoconferencing is taking a practice run. With some effort, videoconferences can ease collaboration on work, regardless of location.[22]

With technology salespeople spending much of their time on the phone simply setting up appointments, opportunities out in the field were being lost. Using cutting-edge technology in sales presentations can be a good way to get sales on the right track. Multimedia presentations—filled with video testimonials from clients, graphics demonstrating your product, and other features—easily can be popped into a client's personal computer (PC) or a laptop for a demonstration and can be a perfect direct mail piece or a leave-behind item after an initial presentation.

Multimedia presentations also allow managers and salespeople in the field to give interactive presentations that formerly might only have been shown in big meetings. Also, by letting the presentation demonstrate the technical details of a product or make a flashy pitch, salespeople can answer specific customer concerns.

The first thing that people think of in bad times is laying off people and cutting programs, and the things that go are the ones that seem experimental. However, often those companies in need of differentiation may be the ones that should consider new media even more.[23]

Developments in technology and communication have allowed personalized solutions for individual customers. Competition is leading companies to treat each customer individually, becoming part of the customer's business processes as an interactive resource.[24]

MODULARITY

Modularity is a strategy for organizing complex products and processes efficiently. A modular system is composed of units (or modules) that are designed independently but still function as an integrated whole. Designers achieve modularity by partitioning information into visible design rules and hidden design parameters. Modularity is beneficial only if the partition is precise, unambiguous, and complete.

The designers of modular systems must know a great deal about the inner workings of the overall product or process to develop the visible design rules necessary to make the modules function as a whole. They have to specify those rules in advance. While designs at the modular level are proceeding independently, it may seem that all is going well; problems with incomplete or imperfect modularization tend to appear only when the modules come together and work poorly as an integrated whole.

Modularity does more than accelerate the pace of change or heighten competitive pressures. It also transforms relations among companies. Module designers rapidly move in and out of joint ventures, technology alliances, subcontracts, employment agreements, and financial arrangements as they compete in a relentless race to innovate. In such markets, revenue and profits are far more dispersed than they would be in traditional industries.

At the same time that modularity boosts the rate of innovation, it also heightens the degree of uncertainty in the design process. There is no way for managers to know which of many experimental approaches will win out in the marketplace. To prepare for sudden and dramatic changes in markets, therefore, managers need to be able to choose from an often complex array of technologies, skills, and financial options.

To compete in a world of modularity, leaders must also redesign their internal organizations. To create superior modules, they need the flexibility to move quickly to market and make use of rapidly changing technologies, but they must also ensure that the modules conform to the architecture. The answer to this dilemma is modularity within the organization. Just as modularity in design boosts innovation in products by freeing designers to experiment, managers can speed up development cycles for individual modules by splitting the work among independent teams, each pursuing a different submodule or different path to improvement.[25]

Companies that make grievous errors in a prosperous industry can still look good on their profit-and-loss statements; thus, they can buy time before a crisis forces change in management practices. By contrast, when the market environment is poor, volatility seems to be much more severe and difficult to resolve.

CRISIS/RISK MANAGEMENT

Crisis of leadership is the onset of the crisis. Who will lead the company out of confusion and solve the managerial problems confronting it? A strong manager is needed—one who has the necessary knowledge and skills to introduce new business techniques. Finding that manager, however, can be difficult. Thus, the first critical choice in an organization's development is to locate and install a strong business manager who is acceptable to senior-level management and who can pull the organization together.[26]

More companies are trying to make a fundamental change in the way they operate (see Figure 5.2). The problem is that the whole burden of change typically rests on so few people. Three concrete interventions will restore companies to vital agility and then keep them in good health: incorporating employees fully into the process

FIGURE 5.2. Reengineering and the Crisis Management Environment

of dealing with business challenges, leading from a different place so as to sharpen and maintain employee involvement and constructive stress, and instilling mental disciplines that will make people behave differently and then helping them sustain their new behavior into the future. Done properly, these three interventions will create a landmark shift in an organization's operating state or culture by significantly altering the way people experience their own power and identity and the way they deal with conflict and learning.

Organizations have similar systems and their vital signs reveal a great deal about their overall health and adaptability, and about the strength and vigor of their functional systems. The following four vital signs give a working definition of culture and tell about the operating state of any company:

- *Power*—Do employees believe they can affect organizational performance? Do they believe they have the power to make things happen?
- *Identity*—Do individuals identify rather narrowly with their professions, working teams, or functional units, or do they identify with the organization as a whole?
- *Conflict*—How do members of the organization handle conflict? Do they smooth problems over, or do they confront and resolve them?

- *Learning*—How does the organization learn? How does it deal with new ideas?

As organizations grow older and larger, however, the vigor of these four vital signs deteriorates. Instead of power, people often develop a sense of resignation in response to seemingly insurmountable obstacles or to lack of support from their superiors in the daily hassle of getting things done. As organizations become more complicated and demanding, people strive to carve out private patches of turf where they can exercise responsibility, protect themselves, and keep the world at bay. When it comes to their identity, therefore, employees lose their sense of teamwork and alignment with the entire enterprise and begin to seek the safety of their particular profession, union, function, team, or location. People in mature organizations tend to avoid conflict for fear of blame or of having someone take their disagreement personally. Alternatively, they may take part in a succession of routine collisions that lead to stalemate rather than resolution. As for learning, larger and older organizations tend to be less receptive to new ideas than their younger counterparts. In place of inquiry and experimentation, ideas get studied to death in hopes of ferreting out every possible weakness before making a commitment.[27] Underestimating uncertainty can lead to strategies that neither defend against the threats nor take advantage of the opportunities that higher levels of uncertainty may provide.

Assuming that the world is entirely unpredictable can lead managers to abandon the analytical rigor of their traditional planning processes altogether and base their strategic decisions primarily on "gut instinct." Risk-averse managers who think they are in very uncertain environments don't trust their gut instincts and suffer from decision paralysis. They avoid making critical strategic decisions about the products, markets, and technologies they should develop. They focus instead on reengineering, quality management, or internal cost-reduction programs. Although valuable, those programs are not substitutes for strategy.

At the heart of the traditional approach to strategy lies the assumption that by applying a set of powerful analytic tools, executives can predict the future of any business accurately enough to allow them to choose a clear strategic direction. In relatively stable businesses, that approach continues to work well. However, it tends to break down when the environment is so uncertain that no amount of good analysis will allow them to predict the future.

Levels of uncertainty regularly confronting managers today are so high that they need a new way to think about strategy.[28] If an organization's culture encourages denial, problems get buried. Corporate cultures are built by successful people, good men and women who are often pillars of their communities as well as business leaders.[29]

As most executives learn in a crisis, the public's reaction to potentially controversial corporate initiatives can be unpredictable. Some companies are tempted to label emotional reactions to corporate initiatives as irrational, and therefore unimportant. Doing so may only provoke an even stronger response from concerned groups and citizens. Some companies are particularly vulnerable to negative publicity because they or other companies in their industry have been linked in the past to questionable practices. Managers in this situation will have to work doubly hard to overcome a tarnished reputation as they move on to new initiatives.

In evaluating a group's strength, companies should judge not only the size of its membership list and war chest but also its internal structure. Many groups, for example, are highly decentralized and slow to act, whereas others are more prepared to take quick action. Companies that attempt to stonewall—or even to squash—rapidly mobilized groups do so at their own risk. A company that jumps out in front on a controversial issue may find itself in deep trouble.

Johnson & Johnson

If managers can defuse potential opposition before it even begins by changing a production process or taking a product off the market, they should. For example, in 1982, Johnson & Johnson made itself a corporate hero by immediately removing Tylenol from store shelves nationwide after a number of bottles were tampered with in the Chicago area.[30]

Johnson & Johnson's handling of the Tylenol crisis is sometimes attributed to the singular personality of then-CEO James Burke. However, the decision to do a nationwide recall of Tylenol capsules to avoid further loss of life from product tampering was, in reality, not one decision but thousands of decisions made by individuals at all levels of the organization. The "Tylenol decision," then, is best understood not as an isolated incident, the achievement of a lone individual, but as the reflection of an organization's culture. Without a shared set of values and guiding principles deeply ingrained throughout the organization, it is doubtful that Johnson & Johnson's response would have been as rapid, cohesive, and ethically sound.[31]

Pepsi-Cola

The numbers at Pepsi-Cola looked great when earnings were up 10 percent, and the business was more profitable in the United States than Coca-Cola's. But projecting in the future, Weatherup, president of a PepsiCo division with sales of over $7 billion, feared that the soda market would turn flat and the competition only get tougher.

Working from headquarters in Somers, New York, Pepsi restructured the organization, redesigned how it did its work, and redefined jobs. The change included breaking the division into 107 customer-focused units and dramatically revising processes such as beverage delivery and special sale promotions, moves that ended up saving Pepsi-Cola tens of millions of dollars. Crisis management is a strategy that corporate leaders can use to radically transform a successful and profitable company before its success and overconfidence and complacency sets in. The idea is based on the familiar phenomenon that most organizations, similar to most people, will not change fundamentally until they absolutely have to.

Effective managers do not wait for a crisis to overtake them. They forsee it and tell other employees about it so that everybody becomes concerned. Then, the leader must give people an idea or vision or picture that allows them to do something about the crisis. In most cases, this means offering people a plan, plus the resources, time, and trust, to address the crisis and devise solutions.

In many instances, only a catastrophe, a new competitor, huge losses, eroding market share, or shrinking revenues, can trigger change. At that point, the price of change can be high. It can mean that thousands of workers get laid off, stockholders end up losing much of their investment, and management gets downsized.[32]

A much less obvious problem in the crucial area of crisis control is crisis creation. This is a problem more likely to hit crisis-ready organizations than those staffed by the unprepared. People trained for action get restless during quiet periods.[33]

BOARDS AND COUNCIL CONCEPT

Appraising a board's performance can clarify the individual and collective roles and responsibilities of its directors, and better knowledge of what is expected of them can help boards become more effective. Although no one can yet show a direct link between a board's effectiveness and its company's profits, improved board performance translates into better corporate governance.

A survey of directors at Fortune 1000 companies conducted in 1996 by Korn/Ferry International indicates that even though roughly 70 percent of the largest U.S. companies have adopted a formal process for evaluating their CEOs, only one-quarter evaluate their boards' performance. Evaluations of individual directors are even rarer and more controversial, occurring in just 16 percent of the companies surveyed.[34]

What is happening is a reversal of the decades-old tendency of corporate power to gather in the hands of executive officers rather than directors or owners, a reversal that will change corporate America for a long time.

In most corporations, CEO accountability was always leading back to the big office to the person who headed the board that judged him or her. Strict federal rules barred shareholders from acting jointly to influence management.

An important reason boards are finally being used effectively is that a spotlight is on them as never before, exposing directors to embarrassment or even lawsuits if they do not perform their jobs.[35]

Practical Use of Boards

Performance reviews may be routine at lower levels of corporations, but they are still a rarity at the top. When boards do conduct reviews, they often focus on executive pay rather than issues such as leadership and effectiveness. Now, more boards are getting the message about reviews and are starting to perform a "sort of corporate hazing" each year on their CEOs. Such appraisals can help the company build tremendous understanding with its board, and some of the feedback can be important.[36]

Is the CEO or president drawing the best out of the employees?

Directors can use a questionnaire form that focuses on four key areas: the company's performance, leadership of the organization, team building and management succession, and leadership of external constituencies, such as customers. Most questions can use a scale from one (definitely not) to seven (definitely yes) to evaluate senior-level executives, but directors should be urged to avoid the fours and "take a position."[37]

BUSINESS AGILITY

For effective performance in a volatile marketplace, people must have strong social skills consistent with the intensely cooperative, team-based environment of agile competition. *Agile competition* refers to the ability to adjust to, adapt to, and anticipate changes that occur in the business environment. Agility also involves a capability to be responsive to a corporate culture that encourages employees to think like owners and share responsibility for the success of the company. It means being flexible in the face of changing work assignments and participating in teams when necessary.[38]

CASE STUDY

Okan Group

Synopsis

Craig Dinsell's problem is restructuring his Dallas/Fort Worth Sales Office. The Okan Group Department is undergoing a massive reorganization and is focused on both production results and minimizing expenses—doing more with less. He inherited the office in

July 1996. Over the past five to six years, it has produced approximately $30 million in new revenue annually. His job is to take the same number of employees and produce $40 million to $50 million in 1997, $60 million to $70 million in 1998, and approximately $100 million in 1999.

Background

Okan is broken into several different business units. Craig works as the Director of Sales for North and West Texas. Okan sells employer-based or group-based medical, dental, life, and disability employee benefits. In today's world, its most recognized products are HMOs and PPOs (managed care).

Okan currently has approximately forty sales offices in the United States. Craig's offices are responsible for approximately $300 million of annual revenue. The Dallas/Fort Worth office consistently ranks in the lower half of the top ten offices within our organization. Expectations are for this office to move consistently into the top five.

Problem to Be Addressed

As described above, this is doing more with less!

Craig's issue is producing with a group of people who have not felt empowered or capable of effecting results. As a whole, the group is cynical and without clear direction. In a short period of time, Okan must get focused, raise the bar, and be organized to produce improved results.

Alternative Solutions

Following are several things that Craig has tried since transferring to Dallas last July:

- Hired an office manager with bottom-line focus and high expectations of himself.
- Recruited "best in class" sales and service representatives.
- Demanded that all new hires, whether clerical or professional, have a "fire in their belly." Craig's approach is basically that

he will hire a word processor who cannot type before he will hire a word processor without a desire to be successful.
- Reorganized the office into a team approach.
- Demanded that employees not allow voice mail to answer their phones, but rather that employees answer their phones with a smile and the ability to solve issues efficiently.

Input

Basically, Craig needs assistance in convincing his staff that answering the telephone quickly and effectively is job number one. Furthermore, he must sell his staff on adding value where they can and not worrying about what they cannot control. They need to be focused on being part of the solution, not part of the problem. They need to believe the glass is half full, not half empty.

Craig needs a structure that will allow the sales representatives to sell 90 percent of the time, the service representatives to proactively service their clients, internal service staff to value their position and take pride in answering the phone and resolving issues, and a support staff that value working for their associates and realize how important their role is to Okan's success

Other Relevant Information

Craig does not have any restrictions as far as participants, nor does he have any preferences toward targeted participants.

An ideal resolution to his situation would provide him with an organizational structure utilizing current staff where possible. He is willing to replace staff if that is his only option for success. One of his more fundamental concerns is the staff answering the phones: Craig has people overqualified for the position and people not quite ready for this level of customer interaction and problem resolution. He has tried giving individuals the opportunity to step up (the underqualified employees) and is currently evaluating the possibility of using his overqualified employees. As is predictable, these individuals are concerned with doing work for which they are overqualified.

Can any of the new management tools help Craig with his situation? Explain.

SECTION III:
STRATEGIC DEVELOPMENTS

Chapter 6

Organizational Communication

INTRODUCTION

A *process* can be as narrowly defined as a single activity in a single function or as broadly defined as the entire business system for the business unit. Effective organizational communication is essential to any reengineering effort. Although the reengineering of single activities or functions can be important to companies with limited problems, a narrow approach to redesign cannot produce the kind of widespread results that many companies seek, without focused communication taking place. Process breadth is important for two reasons. First, if more activities are included in the process, the improvements are more likely to extend throughout the entire business unit. Second, if a process includes interrelated activities, a company may identify incremental opportunities that would not surface in single-function performance improvement efforts. Such opportunities include removing delays and errors in handoffs between functional areas, eliminating problems caused upstream of an activity, and, finally, combining steps that span business units or functions. Many reengineering efforts fail because of insufficient process breadth. The process, in short, is too narrowly defined to have any significant impact on business unit performance as a whole. Still other reengineering efforts fail because of a too broad, indiscriminate approach. Indeed, a diagnostic phase is critical to a company's ability to deliver value to its customers and the bottom line. The key is to identify which two or three elements make up customer value, as well as what defines the company's ability to deliver value to its customers and the bottom line. The next step is to focus on the processes in those areas which fall short of customer expectations, management aspirations, and competitor performance. Organizational communication helps this to occur.

REENGINEERING GOALS

Organizations cannot wait for incremental improvement; they need dramatic breakthroughs to compete in today's business environment. To achieve such breakthroughs, it is necessary to reexamine traditional thinking. Reengineering is built on the notion of busting existing models and thinking. It means wiping the slate totally clean and starting from scratch. It is accompanied by dramatic, order-of-magnitude improvements gained through reinventing the way in which the work is accomplished. It is this promise of radical improvement that makes reengineering so different and so compelling. (See Figure 6.1 for the path to achieving reengineering goals.)

Reengineering is about finding or inventing better ways to give customers what they want, while simultaneously achieving huge gains in performance and productivity (see Figure 6.2). The focus is on finding the best, most efficient way to deliver what customers want—and this focus lands squarely on core processes. Core processes create a product or service of value to external customers. They are a key source of competitive advantage, and improving them can dramatically affect the bottom line.

The human side of reengineering has many common elements: a clear vision of the future, new workplace values and culture, high involvement leadership, full-speed-ahead teams, new workforce skills, customer-driven processes, and new selection and promotion criteria and systems. These common elements can be grouped into three components: culture change; analysis, assessment, and selection; and training and development. The first involves deciding where the organization should go (vision), what it must do to get there (critical success factors), how it will get there (values), and what strategies it will employ to get there. Analysis, assessment, and selection involve identifying skills and abilities needed to support the reengineered process, assessing candidates for the new positions, and selecting the best people to fill those positions. Training and development build the skills people need to implement the reengineered process successfully.

Correctly linking the three components to the technical sides of reengineering is vitally important. There are eight components on the technical side. During targeting, the first component, core pro-

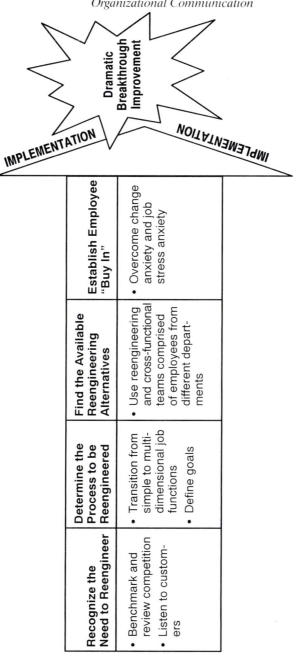

FIGURE 6.1. Steps to Achieving Effective Reengineering

FIGURE 6.2. Radical Redesign of Business Processes to Achieve Breakthrough Result Differences in Corporate Change Strategies

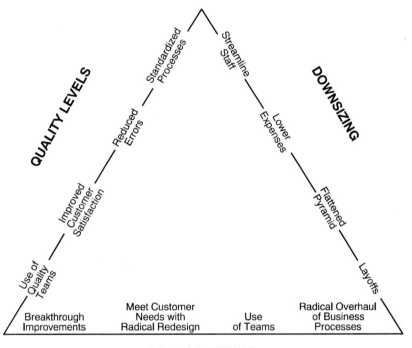

cesses, is identified and selected for reengineering. Baselining, the second component, results in a better understanding of the current process. The third component, innovation, creates new process models, and the fourth, reality checks, gets feedback from customers on the new models. In design, the fifth component, the new process model is developed in detail. During planning, the sixth component, implementation plans are made. The process is piloted in deployment, the seventh component, with full-scale change in transformation, the final component.

When linking culture change to reengineering, every step between the human side and the technical side is inseparable. The

vision and values drive the entire effort, high-involvement strategies flow through all of the steps, and the thrusts for change must be
aligned to make the whole effort work. Although the links to analysis, assessment, and selection do not show up until the later phases
of reengineering, they are critical to successful reengineering efforts. The assessment and selection system design is critical for
selecting the right personnel and putting together and executing
development plans. Development planning occurs in the final three
phases of the technical side of the reengineering effort.

Training and development play an important role throughout the
entire effort, with major emphasis in the early and late phases of
reengineering. Frequently, reengineering results in a shift from a
function-driven, layered organization into a team-based, flat organization designed around teams of people who work throughout the
process. All these changes require new skills for people at all levels
of the organization. Without new leadership skills, involvement,
systems alignment, and the right people with the right skills in the
right jobs, even the best technically reengineered process is doomed
to failure.[1] Employee participation will play an essential role in
management.[2]

BUSINESS COMMUNICATION

Companies always underestimate the level of communication
that must occur during the implementation stage. They tend to use
only one method of communication, such as memos, speeches, or
public relations (PR) videos. More often than not, they neglect the
more time-consuming, but effective, small group format in which
employees can give feedback and air their concerns. It is essential to
create a comprehensive communications program that uses a variety of methods of communication. It helps to assign a top-level
manager to develop and implement an ongoing communications
program. In any redesign project, senior executives must overcome
resistance and convince employees of the need for change.

Once top-level managers have resisted the temptations to stick
with the status quo and have dedicated themselves and their best
performers to the project, they must take a crucial step. By communicating openly, using a variety of methods, managers will encourage

frank discussion, build consensus and commitment, ensure a common understanding of the need for change, foster participative problem solving, celebrate and reinforce accomplishments, and make continuous improvement a company value. Managers must approach communication as an interpersonal activity.

Managers must give employees sound reasons for, and explanations of, the new design, a forum for voicing concerns, and feedback to show those concerns are being heard. This kind of two-way communication will help create champions of the new design throughout all levels of the organization. The successful redesign of a broad process requires the complete restructuring of the key drivers of behavior so that actual results measure up to the redesign plan on paper. Depth means how roles and responsibilities, measurements and incentives, organizational structure, information technology, shared values, and skills change as a result of reengineering.

An effective reengineering transformation requires a *clean slate* approach to process redesign. Only then can companies avoid the classic reengineering pitfall of focusing on fixing the status quo. If the redesign plans are sufficiently broad, all the old support systems will become obsolete—from information technology systems to employee skills. Starting from scratch, companies can plan and build the new infrastructure required to realize the new design. This new infrastructure should include programs such as comprehensive training and skill development plans that require years, not merely months, for success; performance measurement systems that track how well the organization is meeting its targets and how employees should be rewarded based on those objectives; communication programs that help employees understand why and how their behavior must change; information technology development plans that capture the benefits of new technology at a minimal investment, while long-term structural changes are being made. Even with sufficient breadth and depth, a reengineering project will fail without the full commitment of senior executives.

In the most successful redesigns, managers made few compromises and were generous with resources. They saw implementation not as a once-and-for-all effort but as a series of waves washing over the organization for a period of years, leaving a system for continuous improvement in place. Most important, these executives invested their own time in the project. In the six reengineering projects that had significant business cost reductions, top executives spent between 20 percent and 60 percent of their time on the project. In contrast, a manager at a less successful company described the leadership of its process redesign as having "the nominal sponsorship of someone two layers down in the organization, but in actuality, it was driven by someone four layers down. The ultimate redesign ended up focusing on narrow contract and back-office sales processes and never really went anywhere in terms of implementation."[3]

EFFECTIVE COMMUNICATION

The latest writings on competitive skills in academic research and practitioner journals that refer to reengineering, building learning organizations, designing new organizational architectures, managing workforce diversity, and competing globally recognize the importance of business communication skills, both written and verbal; out of a list of twenty-five attributes, these skills were named most important.[4] Other interpersonal skills named by corporations as the most desirable include the following: establishing and maintaining effective working relationships; understanding, evaluating, influencing,. and motivating others; maintaining self-control and objectivity under pressure, especially in dealing with conflict and adversity; and being receptive to feedback.[5] Other research studies also show that firms give hiring priority to communicating effectively.[6]

Importance of Business Communication

Business communication is not a luxury, but a bona fide qualification for effective job performance (see Table 6.1). To remain competitive, organizations must have responsive systems for sharing information and getting work done. Through communication, management is charged to trust employees and employees are encouraged to discuss job-related concerns with bosses. It is important to be aware of the chain of command or employment levels in an organization or customer contract outside of the organization, for effective organizational communication (see Table 6.2). Without organizational relationships, it is tougher for work to get done, or if it is done, it will be slowly.

TABLE 6.1. Business Communication

Importance of Business Communication
1. Research
2. Profit motive
3. Time constraints
4. Hierarchy/chain of command
5. Information
6. Performance
7. Knowledge

TABLE 6.2. Organizational Communication

Role of Organizational Communication Research Findings
Organizational Communication Is Directional:
1. Manager
2. Subordinates
3. Peers
4. Customers

Communication is used to increase competitiveness and to improve employee morale problems. Employees and managers must effectively use communication to continually develop and renew their organizations and to generate unified commitment, encourage a collaborative climate, develop results, and set standards of excellence.

When communicating with:

1. manager—keep boss informed, be loyal, adjust to manager's style, build relationships;
2. subordinates—be an open, empathetic listener, do not reprimand in public, try to build trust and support; you do not have to hit people over the head with your power;
3. peers—use as natural allies that can provide support and informal work groups that enhance or inhibit morale;
4. customers—listen to them, understand their needs and wants, provide top-quality service levels, provide customer satisfaction.

BUSINESS MEETINGS

Most executives spend one- to two-thirds of their time in meetings, and most consider them unproductive.

Planning

1. Identify the purpose. Is it necessary?
2. Prepare an agenda to highlight topics of discussion.
3. Decide who should attend. What can they contribute—status, knowledge about issue, communication skills? Do they have any hidden agendas (ulterior motives—good or bad)?

Conducting

1. Someone leads the meeting—keep the group focused and encourage participation.
2. Start on time (unless a high-level member is late).
3. Follow the agenda.

Follow-Up

1. Determine plan of action to implement.
2. Send out short memo as to what was decided or minutes of the meeting.
3. Make some agreement or statement as to what future actions will be taken.

BUSINESS RESEARCH

Good, sound, quick decision making requires relevant information. Research is a systematic method for obtaining this. Any goal-oriented organization uses this method to facilitate decision making.

Various functional areas in organizations use business research such as accounting to monitor procedures, decisions, and marketing for market share and buyer behavior, personnel for hiring, and managers for goals and performance.

The method used for business research is the scientific method. This asks a scientific proposition and then generates empirical evidence, which is objective, observable, and verifiable, to test the hypothesis to see if it is consistent with the proposition.

Stages

1. Problem.
2. Design—select data source (primary/secondary) and propose cost, supplies, services, time frame.
3. Gather data.
4. Analyze data (in computer, manually, calculate figures).
5. Develop conclusions—data drive conclusions.

EMPOWERMENT

Sharing information is a necessary precondition to another important feature found in many successful work systems: encouraging the decentralization of decision making and broader worker participation and empowerment in controlling their own process.

Organizations that have tapped the power of teams have often experienced excellent results. Teams work because of the peer monitoring and expectations of co-workers that are brought to bear to both coordinate and monitor work. Indeed, even critics of the team concept often argue that the problem with teams as a substitute for hierarchy is not that this approach doesn't work, but that it works too well.

Although the rhetoric of reengineering is consistent with empowerment, in reality, it is anything but that. Both research and practice indicate that the best results of reengineering occur when jobs are rigorously specified and not when individuals are left to define them. Reengineering has led to improvements in performance, but it has not produced the number of highly motivated employees needed to ensure consistently high-performing organizations.

Employees are often ambivalent about empowerment and feel that it is great as long as they are not held personally accountable. Some 83 percent of the 100 Fortune 500 companies surveyed by Pitney Bowes Management Services have introduced reengineering initiatives. Among the executives surveyed from those firms, 70 percent reported increased employee productivity and 60 percent believed that employees felt empowered as a result of the initiatives. Nonetheless, the largest plurality (38 percent) noted that motivating and encouraging employees to change was the greatest challenge they faced. Most reengineering initiatives were implemented in the areas of manufacturing (82 percent), information systems (61 percent), and customer service (60 percent).[7]

Participation and Empowerment

If management wants employees to take more responsibility for their own destiny, it must encourage the development of *internal commitment*. With internal commitment, individuals are committed to a particular project, person, or program based on their own reasons or motivations. Internal commitment is participatory and very closely allied with empowerment. The more that top management wants an internal commitment from its employees, the more it must try to involve employees in defining work objectives, specifying how to achieve them, and setting stretch targets.

Management says it wants employees who participate more, and employees say they want to be more involved. While employees push for greater autonomy, management says the right thing but tries to keep control through information systems, processes, and tools. It is important to establish working conditions to increase empowerment in the organization. Many employees are willing to become more personally committed if management is sincere and if they can be rewarded.

Although morale, satisfaction, and even commitment should be calculated into human relations policies, the ultimate goal is performance. Individuals can be excellent performers and report low morale, yet it is performance and not morale that is most important. When morale, satisfaction, and a sense of empowerment are used as the ultimate criteria for success in organizations, they cover up many of the problems that organizations must overcome.

Some people do well with all the technical aspects of their job, but fall short in their communications skills. With workers expected to sort out problems among themselves rather than have managers intervene, strong interpersonal skills are vital.[8] When Opinion Research Corporation of Chicago surveyed 100,000 middle managers, supervisors, professionals, salespeople, and technical, clerical, and hourly workers of Fortune 500 companies in 1988, it found that the lines of communications were weak. With the exception of the sales group, employees believed top management now was less willing to listen to their problems than five years earlier.

Foster Higgins & Company, an employee benefits consulting firm, finds that only 45 percent of large employers make regular use of worker opinion surveys, which easily provide employee feedback to management. Towers Perrin, a large consulting firm, after studying Fortune 500 companies' use of a wide variety of from-the-bottom-up communications tools, including surveys, telephone hotlines, quality circles, suggestion programs, and exit interviews, concluded that the communication levels of many corporations were only marginal.

According to a survey by the Forum Corporation, a consulting firm, 82 percent of Fortune 500 executives believe their corporate strategy is understood by "everyone who need to know." In addition, Louis Harris research firm finds that only less than one-third of employees say management provides clear goals and direction. When the Hay Consultant Group asked what kind of information workers wanted more of from top management, employees indicated that "reliable information on where the company is headed" and "how my job fits into the total" were most important.

Although Foster Higgins Research Company finds 97 percent of the CEOs it surveyed believe communicating with employees has a positive impact on job satisfaction, and 79 percent think it benefits the bottom line, only 22 percent actually do it weekly or more often.[9] One definition of morale is "a sense of shared direction where a committed employee is willing to take risks along with the company." If the company says, "We need to change," the employee is willing to undertake the risk.[10]

TEAMS

Increasingly, American managers are being judged not just by those who rule above them but by those who work under them. The new measure of performance, spreading rapidly in the past year or two, is known by various names, most commonly upward evaluation or 360-degree feedback. Executives under review—and in some companies that extends all the way up to the CEO—are often subject to a full circle of criticism as well as praise from subordinates, peers, superiors, and even customers.[11] Managers who dislike conflict—or value only their own approach—actively avoid the clash of ideas. They hire and reward people of a particular type, usually people similar to themselves.[12]

In business organizations, the benefits of high sociability are clear and numerous. First, most employees agree that working in such an environment is enjoyable, which helps morale. Sociability often helps creativity because it fosters teamwork, sharing of information, and a spirit of openness to new ideas and allows the freedom to express and accept out-of-the-box thinking. Sociability also creates an environment in which individuals are more likely to go beyond the formal requirements of their jobs. They work harder than is technically necessary to help their colleagues look good and succeed.

There also are drawbacks to high levels of sociability. The prevalence of friendships may allow poor performance to be tolerated. It is difficult to rebuke or fire a friend. It is more comfortable to accept and excuse subpar performance in light of an employee's personal problems. In addition, high-sociability environments are often characterized by an exaggerated concern for consensus. Friends are often reluctant to disagree with or criticize one another. In business settings, such a tendency can easily lead to diminished debate over goals, strategies, or simply how work gets done.

In addition, high-sociability communities often develop cliques and informal, behind-the-scenes networks that can circumvent or, worse, undermine due process in an organization. This is not to say that high-sociability companies lack formal organizational structures (see Figure 6.3 for an example of team structure). Many of them are very hierarchical. However, friendships and unofficial networks of friendships allow people to pull an end run around the hierarchy.[13]

Teams hobbled by conflict lack common goals. Team members perceive themselves to be in competition with one another and, surprisingly, tend to frame decisions negatively, as reactions to threats. Many studies of group decision making and intergroup conflict demonstrate that common goals build team cohesion by stressing the shared interest of all team members in the outcome of

FIGURE 6.3. Structural Teams to Review, Allocate Resources, and Initiate the Reengineering Effort

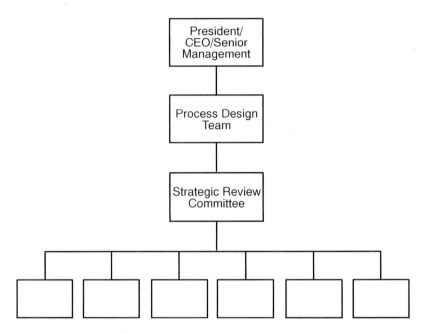

Functional Area Reengineering Teams

the debate. When team members are working toward a common goal, they are less likely to see themselves as individual winners and losers and are far more likely to perceive the opinions of others correctly and to learn from them. Teams that handle conflict well make explicit attempts to relieve tension and, at the same time, promote a collaborative spirit by making their business fun. They emphasize the excitement of fast-paced competition, not the stress of competing in tough and uncertain markets.

Research suggests that autocratic leaders who manage through highly centralized power structures often generate high levels of interpersonal friction. At the other extreme, weak leaders also engender interpersonal conflict. Interpersonal conflict is lowest in balanced power structures, which are those in which the CEO is more powerful than the other members of the top-management team, but the members do wield substantial power, especially in their own well-defined areas of responsibility. In balanced power structures, all executives participate in strategic decision making.

Balancing power is one tactic for building a sense of fairness. Finding an appropriate way to resolve conflict over issues is another—perhaps, the more crucial. Research shows that the teams that managed conflict effectively all used the same approach to resolving substantive conflict. Managers talk over an issue and try to reach consensus. If they can, the decision is made, and if not, the most relevant senior manager makes the decision, guided by input from the rest of the group.

In a team that insists on consensus, deadlines can cause executives to sacrifice fairness and thus weaken the team's support for the final decision. Without conflict, groups lose their effectiveness. Managers often become withdrawn and only superficially harmonious. Teams unable to foster substantive conflict ultimately achieve, on average, lower performance.[14]

What makes some teams so controversial is that they ultimately force managers to give up control. If teams are working right, they manage themselves. A team may arrange schedules, set profit targets, and may even have a say in hiring and firing team members as well as managers, and in some cases, it may devise strategy.

Teams typically consist of between three and thirty workers. In a few cases, they have become a permanent part of the workforce. In others, management assembles the team for a few months or years to develop a new product or solve a particular problem. Companies that use them usually see productivity rise dramatically. Teams make the most sense only if a job entails a high level of dependency among three or more people.

There remains considerable debate among employees, managers, and consultants over the best way to compensate team members. Most companies pay a flat salary. Instead of handing out automatic annual raises, they often use a pay-for-skills system that bases any increase not on seniority but on what an employee has learned. The most common problem is the failure by team members to understand the feelings and needs of their co-workers.[15]

Corporations underestimate the mind-set and behavioral skills that team leaders need. Even the most capable managers have trouble making the transition because the command functions they were encouraged to do before are no longer appropriate. Managers worry that all the soft skills so essential for success as a team leader, such as communication, conflict resolution, and coaching, translate into a promotion within the company or another position elsewhere. As managers turn over more responsibilities to teams, it is only natural for them to wonder if they are empowering themselves right out of a job.[16]

Forming a team, which often groups employees or salespeople with product specialists and support staffers, is not a panacea to improve low revenue or increase market share. One study illustrates the growing number of teams. According to the study, which surveyed primarily Fortune 1000 companies, only 13 percent of the 179 teams researched received high ratings for effectiveness. According to a study by the Hay Group, 30 percent of surveyed mangers said teams failed to meet expectations because they were not supported by the compensation plan.[17]

Leadership

What prevents most organizations from going beyond the ordinary is insufficient leadership capacity. CEOs who think specifically about leadership capacity stand a far better chance of getting their organizations to push through the barriers of normal performance. CEOs should look beyond their senior management group for potential leaders. In the age of reengineering, attrition, early retirement, and right-sizing, many leaders are consigned prematurely to leave the corporation. Enlightened CEOs cannot afford to let these knowledgeable veterans fade away.[18]

Business already is moving to organize itself into virtual corporations, fungible modules built around information networks, flexible workforces, outsourcing, and webs of strategic partnerships. Virtual leadership is about keeping everyone focused as old structures, including old hierarchies, crumble.[19] Good leaders know how to tap the talents each person brings to the team for the good of the company and the individuals.[20]

Contemporary leadership seems to be a matter of aligning people toward common goals and empowering them to take the actions needed to reach them. Ultimately, that means a leader must become worthy of respect.

CASE STUDY

Monarch Wealth Management

Synopsis

Will a unified sales strategy (USS)—same sales force representing three different business units—be a viable solution under an evolving affluent client strategy?

Each business unit has a fair bit of autonomy as long as they meet/exceed their business objectives and operate within some broad guidelines. Although there is acknowledgment by all in select meetings that the USS will work, it is apparent that this is mere lip service based on the repeated actions of a particular business unit that happens to be a key player in this process.

Description of Problem/Issue

Over the last four years, Monarch Wealth Management (MWM) has undergone radical change:

- September 1993, Monarch Bank acquired Monarch Wealth Management.
- Some upheaval occurred in months preceding and following acquisition: clash of cultures, perceptions, merging systems, the usual challenges associated with big mergers, not the least of which was the urgent need to provide strong leadership and resurrect the "outreach sales force," a major distribution channel and core element of the sales strategy.
- September 1994, MWM reorganizes from four regions primarily focused on retail, trust, and investments to ten market centers concentrating on trust, investments, and global private

banking services. Equally important was the challenge to adopt an effective client migration strategy to the bank that was envisaged would handle clients at the lower end of the market spectrum (i.e., those who were primarily transaction focused), freeing up MWM to concentrate on *advice giving* through a host of MWM Services.

- December 1994 to March 1995, discussions take place and senior management gives approval to implement concept of unified sales strategy.
- High priority to turn around performance of sales force and make it the focal point of our delivery of MWM services to the affluent client.
- Samuels Consulting engaged to review compensation model and other broader issues relating to the sales force and make recommendations as to the strategic direction.
- Samuels Consulting recommended fine-tuning the compensation model and endorsed USS.

Relevant Players

The three business units which agreed in principle to the unified sales strategy and which had a common MWM thread are the following:

- Trust (part of MWM)
- Monarch Bank Investment Counsel Incorporated (MBIC)
- Global Private Banking

Current Approach/Solutions Tried

Effective November:

- Reporting Change: VP Sales Management who had previously only reported in to the Senior Vice President MWM has, for the last year, had a dual reporting relationship and reports in to the President of MBIC as well. This change was brought about to enable more direct accountability, better communication, and a shared role in all sales management decisions regarding the advisor sales force.

- VP Sales Management actively participates in all MBIC meetings/conference calls.
- At least one MBIC VP participates in all MWM meetings and our monthly sales management conference calls/quarterly meetings.
- MBIC is involved in the hiring of new advisors.
- Believe that portfolio managers can do a better job selling discretionary investment management services than advisors.
- Maintain that advisors not qualified—track records on sales by advisors prove otherwise.
- Reluctance to share marketing/proposal material/compensation plans is very cost conscious.
- Support, at best, is superficial at national office level, better in the field.

Input from Consultants

As the current MWM business evolves into a more formalized affluent client strategy encompassing other MWM businesses, will the concept of USS be a viable one in this broader context?

What are the key recommendations going forward with regard to organizational communication?

Chapter 7

Professional Development and Learning

INTRODUCTION

Achieving competitive success through people involves fundamentally altering how we think about the workforce and the employment relationship. It means achieving success by working with people, not by replacing them or limiting the scope of their activities. It entails seeing the workforce as a source of strategic advantage, not just as a cost to be minimized or avoided. Firms that take this different perspective are often able to successfully outmaneuver and outperform their rivals. This is what some firms have accomplished through reengineering.

One of the most extensive studies on reengineering was sponsored by Boston University's Manufacturing Roundtable. It covered twenty-three BPR projects and was reported on in the *California Management Review*. The conclusions reached were that BPR incorporates many of the practices of good management that have long been recognized as contributing to better performance, such as the need for management commitment and for appropriate training. The study goes on to say that success in BPR is dependent upon strong leadership and an orientation that focuses efforts on changing direction.[1]

Much of the literature on reengineering has assumed that it is automatically good for an organization. As a consequence, there has been little reportage of actual reengineering failures. Estimates of failure rates vary. It is probably the case that many failures may go unreported since the organization will understandably not want to publicize the fact or, indeed, may not even survive to tell the tale. Therefore, it is likely that the true failure rate may be even higher.

Certainly, many companies only begin to consider reengineering when they are faced with a survival-threatening crisis and radical action is required.[2] Various interrelated practices seem to characterize companies that are effective in achieving competitive success through how they manage people.

EFFECTIVE PRACTICES OF COMPANIES THAT ACHIEVE COMPETITIVE SUCCESS

Mentors

As organizations have become less hierarchical and as more work is done by teams, the definition of mentoring has changed. No longer can a single person be expected to protect, guide, and champion an employee's cause. To succeed today, workers should have many mentors—peers, subordinates, or people outside the company. Both mentor and protégé will benefit from the relationship by improving management skills and having a sense of being valued by the organization, and the protégé by being advised and having a sounding board and role model.

Formal mentoring programs in companies typically match junior employees with those at higher levels above them. Often forgotten, however, are the needs of high-level executives. They may be at the pinnacle of their careers but still crave feedback, support, and advice.

Managers often come into the job with unrealistic expectations, focusing more on the rights and privileges and underestimating the duties and obligations. Effective professional development of subordinates is one of the requirements of a skilled manager. Also, managers tend to focus on managing their immediate subordinates, not realizing they must also manage the perceptions of bosses and managers in other departments, whose support they need to get their jobs done. Some managers also have trouble accepting their changing roles. It is useful to get help from other managers and from contacts outside the company, such as in professional groups.[3]

Employment Security

Security of employment signals a long-standing commitment by the organization to its workforce. Norms of reciprocity tend to guarantee that this commitment is repaid. However, conversely, an employer that signals through word and deed that its employees are dispensable is not likely to generate much loyalty, commitment, or willingness to expend extra effort for the organization's benefit.

Security in employment and reliance on the workforce for competitive success mean that one must be careful to choose the right people in the right way. Studies covering populations ranging from machine operators, typists, and welders to assembly workers—all in self-paced jobs so that individual differences mattered—indicate that the most productive employees were about twice as good as the least productive. Besides getting the right people in the door, recruiting has an important symbolic aspect. If someone goes through a rigorous selection process, the person feels that he or she is joining an elite organization. High expectations for performance are created, and the message sent is that people matter.

High Wages

High wages tend to attract more applicants, permitting the organization to be more selective in finding people who are going to be trainable and who will be committed to the organization. Perhaps most important, higher wages send a message that the organization values its people. Particularly if these wages are higher than required by the market, employees can perceive the extra income as a gift and work more diligently as a result.

There has been a tendency to overuse money in an effort to solve myriad organizational problems. People are motivated by more than money—things such as recognition, security, and fair treatment matter a great deal. Nevertheless, if people are responsible for enhanced levels of performance and profitability, they will want to share in the benefits. Consider the alternative—if all the gains from extra ingenuity and effort go just to top management or to shareholders (unless these are also employees), people will soon view the situation as unfair, become discouraged, and abandon their efforts. Thus, many organizations seek to reward performance with some form of contingent compensation.

Employee Ownership

Employee ownership offers two advantages. Employees who have ownership interests in the organizations for which they work have less conflict between capital and labor—to some degree they are both capital and labor. Employee ownership, effectively implemented, can align the interests of employees with those of shareholders by making employees shareholders too. Second, employee ownership puts stock in the hands of people, the employees, who are more inclined to take a long-term view of the organization, its strategy, and its investment policies and less likely to support hostile takeovers, leveraged buyouts, and other financial maneuvers. Of course, to the extent that one believes this reduced risk of capital market discipline inhibits efficiency, significant employee shareholding is a disadvantage. However, the existing evidence largely contradicts this negative view.

If people are to be the source of competitive advantage, clearly they must have the information necessary to do what is required to be successful.

Training and Skill Development

An integral part of most new work systems is a greater commitment to training and skill development. Note, however, that this training will produce positive returns only if the trained workers are then permitted to employ their skills.

Having people do multiple jobs has a number of potential benefits. The most obvious is that doing more things can make work more interesting—variety is one of the core job dimensions that affect how people respond to their work. Variety in jobs permits a change in pace, a change in activity, and potentially even a change in the people with whom one comes in contact, and each of these forms of variety can make work life more challenging. Beyond its motivational effects, having people do multiple jobs has other important benefits. One is keeping the work process both transparent and as simple as possible. If people are expected to shift to new tasks readily, the design of those tasks has to be straightforward enough so that they can be learned quickly. A second, somewhat related benefit is the potential for newcomers to a job to see things that can be improved that experienced people don't see, simply because they have come to take the work process so much for granted.

Promotion from Within

Promotion from within is a useful adjunct to many of the practices described. It encourages training and skill development because the availability of promotion opportunities within the firm binds workers to employers and vice versa. It facilitates decentralization, participation, and delegation because it helps promote trust across hierarchical levels; promotion from within means that supervisors are responsible for coordinating the efforts of people whom they probably know quite well. By the same token, those being coordinated personally know managers in higher positions. This contact provides social bases of influence so that formal position can loom less important.

The bad news about achieving some competitive advantage through the workforce is that it inevitably takes time to accomplish. By contrast, a new piece of equipment can be quickly installed; a new product technology can be acquired through a licensing agreement in the time it takes to negotiate the agreement; and acquiring capital only requires the successful conclusion of negotiations. The good news, however, is that once achieved, competitive advantage obtained through employment practices is likely to be substantially more enduring and more difficult to duplicate. Nevertheless, the time required to implement these practices and start seeing results means that a long-term perspective is needed. It also takes a long time horizon to execute many of these approaches. In the short term, laying off people is probably more profitable compared to trying to maintain employment security; cutting training is a quick way to maintain short-term profits; and cross-training and cross-utilization may provide insights and innovation in time, but initially, the organization foregoes the advantages of more narrow specialization and the immediate proficiency achieved thereby.

PERFORMANCE MEASUREMENT SYSTEMS

The design of any performance measurement system should reflect the basic operating assumptions of the organization it supports. If the organization changes and the measurement system does not, the latter will be, at best, ineffective or, more likely, counterproductive. With many companies that have moved from control-oriented, functional hierarchies to a faster and flatter team-based approach, traditional performance measurement systems not only fail to support the new teams but also undermine them.

The primary role of traditional measurement systems, which are still used in most companies, is to pull good information up so that senior managers can make good decisions that flow down. To that end, each relatively independent function has its own set of measures, whose main purpose is to inform top managers about the function's activities. Marketing tracks market share, operations watches inventory, and finance monitors costs.

Measurement systems tell an organization where it stands in its effort to achieve goals, but not how it got there. Most results measures track what goes on within a function, not what happens across functions. The few cross-functional results measures in organizations are typically financial, such as revenues, gross margins, costs of goods sold, capital assets, and debt, and they exist only to help top managers. In contrast, process measures monitor the tasks and activities throughout an organization that produce a given result. Such measures are essential for cross-functional teams that are responsible for processes that deliver an entire service or product to customers, such as order fulfillment or new product development.

The main purpose of a measurement system should be to help a team. A truly empowered team must play the lead role in designing its own measurement system. A team should know what sort of measurement system it needs, but the team should not design this system in isolation.[4]

MEASUREMENT

Measurement is a critical component in any management process, and this is true for the process of managing the organization's workforce. Measurement serves several functions. First, it provides feedback as to how well the organization is implementing various policies. For example, many organizations espouse a promotion from within policy but do not fulfill this objective. Often, this is because there is no systematic collection and reporting of information, such as what percentage of the positions at given levels have been filled internally. A commitment to a high-wage policy obviously requires information as to where in the relevant labor market the organization's wages fall. A commitment to training is more likely to be fulfilled if data are collected, not only on the total amount spent on training, but also on what types of employees have received training and what sorts of training are being delivered.

Second, measurement ensures that what is measured will be noticed. "Out of sight, out of mind" is a principle that applies to organizational goals and practices, as well as to people. One of the most consistent findings in organizational literature is that measures affect behavior. Most people will try to succeed on the measures even if there are no direct, immediate consequences. Things that are measured get talked about, and things that are not do not.[5]

An outstanding corporate strategy is not a random collection of individual building blocks, but a carefully constructed system of interdependent parts. More than a powerful idea, it actively directs executives' decisions about the resources the corporation will develop, the businesses the corporation will compete in, and the organization that will make it all come to life. A great corporate strategy begins with a vision of how a company's resources will differentiate it from competitors across multiple businesses. It must also articulate how to achieve that vision. In particular, what kinds of coordination and control must the company provide to effectively deploy its resources?

Most corporate-level executives understand the need to add value to their businesses, yet few put in place the organizational mechanisms to make that possible. Many executives are reluctant to violate the autonomy and accountability of independent business units. Others fear they will end up with large bureaucratic overhead structures. Companies, however, achieve the benefits of coordination with modest organizational costs.[6]

Apple was forced to introduce a reengineered version of the Newton Message Pad after the first one failed.[7] Companies that succeed today do much more than make incremental changes to existing systems. Reengineering a business requires breakthrough thinking by everyone in the organization. It involves employing new technology and innovative processes, empowering people to take on greater responsibility at all levels, and forging new strategic alliances with vendors and outside suppliers to gain a competitive advantage in the marketplace.

Taco Bell places the decision-making processes directly in the hands of their dine-in and drive-through customers with computer-touch screen-ordering technology. In the food service business today, consumers define value in terms of quality, fair prices, *and* convenience.[8]

After a major downsizing crisis, many companies seem to stumble along, oblivious to the lessons of the past. Employee surveys often are used to gather information and opinions about major events that have shaken up a business, but the assembled data rarely make it back to the organization's people in a form they can use meaningfully. Best practice write-ups leave out the mistakes that people might learn from, as well as the hidden logic and struggles that have made breakthroughs possible.

In reengineering, redesign, or other change initiatives, the most critical factor for success is the quality of human interaction in the organization—which often depends on the humility and openness of the leaders who direct the effort.[9]

The dominant factor for business in the next two decades will be demographics. The key factor for business will be the increasing *under*population of the developed countries—Japan and the nations of Europe and North America. The number of college and university students in all of China, which has a population of 1.25 billion, is no more than 3 million. Compare that figure with the 12.5 million students in the United States, which has one-fifth of China's population. To convert this quantitative lead into a qualitative lead is one, and perhaps the only, way for developed countries to maintain their competitive position in the world economy. This means continual, systematic work on the productivity of knowledge and knowledge workers, which is still neglected and abysmally low.[10]

Executives will be forced to rethink the *strategic* fundamentals of their businesses. Within a corporation, traditional concepts of span of control and hierarchical reporting are predicated on the belief that jobs are structured to channel communication among a few people standing in a hierarchical relationship to one another, and broader communication is effected through the indirect routes of the organizational pyramid. One entire economic theory suggests that the boundaries of the corporation are set by the economics of exchanging information: organizations enable the exchange of information among a narrow, internal group; markets enable the exchange of information among a larger, external group. The point at which one mode becomes less cost-effective than the other determines the boundaries of the corporation.

The emergence of universal technical standards for communication, allowing everybody to communicate at zero cost, underlie all the Net technologies: the *Internet*, which connects everyone; *extranets*, which connect companies to one another; and *intranets*, which connect individuals within companies.[11] The essential problem in organizations today is a failure to distinguish *planning* from *strategizing*. Planning is about programming, not discovering. Strategizing is not a rote procedure—it is a quest.[12] The scarcest resources in any enterprise are people who are knowledgeable, experienced, forward looking, and able to lead. When a team and its leader are in place, it is time to turn to the first target of the evaluation process: customers. Having grouped customers, products, and services, it is time to get down to the nitty-gritty of the strategic renewal process by evaluating them individually for their strategic importance, significance, and profitability.[13]

A well-written narrative strategy that provides a difficult situation with an innovative solution leading to improved market share can be galvanizing—and it is certainly more engaging than a bulleted mandate to "increase market share by 5 percent." When people can locate themselves in the story, their sense of commitment and involvement is enhanced.[14]

LEARNING ORGANIZATION

Most scholars view organizational learning as a process that unfolds over time and link it with knowledge acquisition and improved performance. A *learning organization* is an organization skilled at creating, acquiring, and transferring knowledge and at modifying its behavior to reflect new knowledge and insights. Learning organizations are skilled at five main activities: systematic problem solving, experimentation with new approaches, learning from their own experience and past history, learning from the experiences and best practices of others, and transferring knowledge quickly and efficiently throughout the organization.

The most effective training programs are tightly focused and feature a small set of techniques tailored to employees' needs. Training in design of experiments, for example, is useful for manufacturing engineers, whereas creativity techniques are well suited to development groups. Not all learning comes from reflection and self-analysis. Sometimes the most powerful insights come from looking outside one's immediate environment to gain a new perspective. Enlightened managers know that even companies in completely different businesses can be fertile sources of ideas and catalysts for creative thinking.

Benchmarking

Benchmarking is an ongoing investigation and learning experience that ensures that best industry practices are uncovered, analyzed, adopted, and implemented (see Figure 7.1). The greatest benefits come from studying practices, the way that work gets done, rather than results, and from involving line managers in the process. Almost anything can be benchmarked. Customers can provide up-to-date product information, competitive comparisons, insights into

FIGURE 7.1. Organizational Learning and Benchmarking

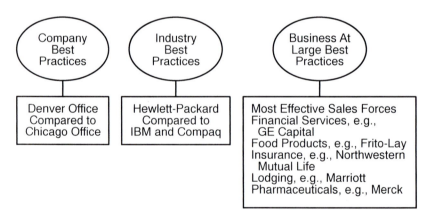

Source: Based on B. Keenan "Best Sales Force Ratings," *Sales & Marketing Management Magazine* (July 1998), p. 24.

changing preferences, and immediate feedback about service and patterns of use. Institutional learning is the process through which management teams change their shared mental models of their company, their markets, and their competitors. Companies are increasingly outsourcing strategic planning. Disappointed with the high cost and low productivity of their internal strategic planning staff, they are leaning on consulting firms for advice on strategic direction rather than developing strategic thinking as a core competence for their senior executives.[15]

Executive Management Education

For example, top universities, such as Harvard, Stanford, Columbia, and Virginia, are scrambling to keep up with new thinking about just what executive education is supposed to accomplish. Dozens of business schools are spending months devising elaborate, half-million-dollar customized courses that will be given only to employees of a particular company. The programs, at $32,000 a pop for Harvard's flagship Advanced Management Program, remain enormously profitable for the institutions.

Foreign executives are also participating, comprising slack: they are two-thirds of the students at Harvard's AMP, up from one-third ten years ago. Students from overseas occupy about half the seats at advanced management courses at Stanford and Columbia too.

Columbia University has highly successful programs in both sales and marketing management that allow line managers to upgrade their skills in these areas. They are also able to learn cutting-edge strategic and practical ideas that they can bring back to their organizations for competitive advantage. Columbia's Sales Management Program does this by using faculty with research management and consulting backgrounds who can draw from their own expertise in leadership, negotiation, planning, sales strategy, and crisis management to keep management participants current.

The approach to executive education that is probably getting the most attention these days is action learning. It works by giving teams of executives real live business problems to solve. The business problems are identified by the company's top officials. Preparing them are consultants and B-school professors who teach them new ways of organizing, thinking, and deciding before they complete the program.

Some of these executive programs care primarily about getting high ratings from participants on the last day of class, so they design programs that are entertaining instead of useful.[16] However, many executive education programs fulfill their role by giving managers insights and skills that help them execute the strategy of the company.

PART-TIME EMPLOYMENT

The model of long-term employment is dead and buried. Nearly 45 million people, more than one-third of the American workforce, are either self-employed or working as temps, part-timers, or consultants. This contingent workforce has grown 57 percent since 1980, three times faster than the labor force as a whole.

For a fast-growing number of managers and professionals, work is now a combination of stints, ranging from two weeks to two years. This phenomenon, known variously as interim management, professional assignment, or even head renting, is growing faster than anyone can track it. *Executive Recruiter* estimates that at least 125,000 professionals labor as temps every day. These numbers do not include the thousands of managers who classify themselves as self-employed consultants.

Networking with colleagues, friends, neighbors, customers, suppliers, and acquaintances is one of the keys to remaining employable. Research shows that most people find new jobs not by sending out résumés or responding to want ads but by using connections—in other words, by networking. Network meetings are a way to stay current in a profession.

When the volatility of the corporate world seems unbearable, some managers try starting their own business, which under the circumstances may provide more stability.[17] Career counselors say there are two kinds of networking: inside a company and outside the organization. Counselors caution against taking a tunnel-vision approach to networking outside the workplace. Although trade associations and professional organizations are important, do not overlook people who share personal interests as potentially valuable ways to make contacts.[18] Supporters argue that greater use of contingent workers, by increasing companies' flexibility, lowering costs, and lifting competitiveness, will enable them to provide greater job security—and fatter paychecks—for the far larger number of permanent workers who remain.

What troubles a vocal minority of business leaders is the devastating effect the temping of the workforce can have on incomes, mental health, and even the social fabric. Having many part-time workers does not create the loyalty and ownership of results that being a regular part of the team does.[19] For most Americans, the workplace has become a far more capricious place. During the past decade, corporate America has restructured, downsized, right-sized, and reengineered millions of people out of their jobs, while putting the squeeze on wages of remaining workers.

The restructuring of corporate America has carried enormous social costs. Today, corporations essentially all have the same technology, the same networking systems, and the same software. The only way they can beat out their competitors is by enabling their biggest asset, their workforce, to be more innovative in using the technology to create new products and new services that sell well. Instead, throughout its decade-long restructuring, corporate America has primarily viewed workers as liabilities rather than assets.

For corporations, that means better training programs, heightened sensitivity to the anguish of layoffs, and shared sacrifice by management.[20] Too many Americans lack the skills needed to flourish in the laser-fast, high-performance, totally empowered, fully global world. American companies have got to be urged to treat their workers as assets to be developed rather than as costs to be cut.[21]

CASE STUDY

Serxner Bank

Synopsis

- Effectively reinforce a sales culture among five regional sales managers who are widely dispersed across Canada.
- Ensure that team members understand and agree upon a common sense of purpose and understand how their actions will guide the group in achieving its intended goals.

Background

The Serxner Bank is one of California's largest banks and employs more than 25,000 people. The bank maintains 910 branches and 1,996 ATMs across the state. At the end of the third quarter, fiscal 1997 (July 31, 1997), Serxner Bank had $156.1 billion in assets under management.

The Personal Lending Group consists of twenty people who are divided into teams that are responsible for sales, marketing, product delivery, product development, and risk management of personal lending (loans and lines of credit). The group is led by the Vice President, Personal Lending Group. The group's mission is to achieve best sales results, best delivery, and provide best solutions to become the leader in personal lending in California.

Heading for Problem to Be Addressed

How can the company continuously reinforce a sales culture to ensure that branch sales team members work toward a common purpose?

Description of Issue

National Branch Sales position was created in September 1996. Two regional sales managers (RSMs) were hired in March 1997. They were recruited directly from branches located in the division in which they currently function. They operate in divisions located within several hours drive from the corporate head office. (Depending upon geographic area, bank branches are located in one of eight divisions.)

The RSMs' responsibilities focus on working very closely with divisional, regional, and branch management to conduct the following activities:

- Establish an active call program among targeted branches within a division (represents 30 percent of total branches within a division, or approximately thirty-five to fifty branches that have been identified as high potential and low sales volumes).

- Provide credit sales training.
- Establish regional sales competitions.
- Promote best sales practices among regions.
- Develop regional marketing programs that focus upon increasing penetration among existing households.

The RSMs are evaluated on sales performance that is incremental to direct branch sales. The level of incremental sales corresponds to attaining a multiple of the RSMs' total compensation.

Prior to commencing these activities, the RSMs participated in a training program over four weeks. Training provided the RSMs with an in-depth understanding of the strategy of the Personal Lending Group, the importance of their role, and their measurable goals. As well, training provided technical skills (e.g., presentation skills, software applications) to ensure that the RSMs would efficiently and confidently accomplish their goals.

Bi-weekly meetings are held between the manager and National Branch Sales to resolve issues, celebrate successes, and measure sales performance against goals. As well, quarterly joint sales calls are made with the RSM and the Manager, National Branch Sales. Weekly meetings are held among the Personal Lending Group and the RSM via conference call.

Three additional RSMs will be hired over the next two months. Two RSMs will be located on the West Coast, and one RSM will be located a significant distance northeast of the corporate head office.

As the sales force expands and becomes more geographically dispersed, the continuous reinforcement of the sales culture, including focusing on a common sense of purpose, will become more difficult to attain. Furthermore, the RSMs have more regular contact with divisional and regional management than the Personal Lending Group. The sense of purpose and values is different between divisional/regional management and the Personal Lending Group. How can Serxner Bank continuously focus their attention on the shared purpose and motivate them to work toward the team's goals?

Alternate Solutions

- Increase regular communication.
- Increase joint sales calls.

Input Requested

- Key successes of national sales managers who manage a geographically dispersed group.
- Implementation process to develop a continuously reinforcing sales culture.

:

SECTION IV:
EXAMINATION OF VARIOUS
ORGANIZATIONS AND
REENGINEERING

Chapter 8

An Evaluation of Best Practices Resulting from Reengineering

INTRODUCTION

Some research suggests that, although there are some success stories, most reengineering efforts have only yielded high costs, high turnover, cynical and rebellious workers, and, in the worst cases, further reorganization through Chapter 11 bankruptcy.[1]

It is incorrect to assume that all reengineering changes must be of large magnitude. Many industry surveys show that a majority of reengineering projects are incremental, rather than radical, in nature. Analysis suggests that a piecemeal approach, involving incremental changes heading in the right direction, can be a rational response to budget constraints and unfavorable organizational and technological conditions.[2]

Between 1990 and 1995, Cigna, the insurance company, reduced its workforce by 25 percent and IBM took its employee base of 400,000 down by 33 percent. GE lowered its workforce by over 200,000, and Procter & Gamble instituted a 12 percent employee reduction, while increasing sales.[3] The following examples will look at best practices resulting from reengineering.

AT&T

Since divestiture on January 1, 1984, AT&T has shed 140,000 jobs, lost nearly 30 percent of the long distance market to upstarts such as MCI and Sprint, and struggled fitfully to make it in the computer business. However, it has also uprooted its complacent, sluggish, inward-looking culture.

With these changes, AT&T has

- installed a new corporate structure that encourages cooperation among otherwise independent businesses, including cross-unit teams that forage for new opportunities;
- spent huge amounts of time promoting a set of company values, among which are respect for individuals and dedication to helping customers;
- shaken up the organization and ended a tradition of insularity by recruiting executives from outside; and
- invested in other companies with critical technologies or attractive market positions.

Every AT&T business unit now has two mandates: grow and be profitable in your own right, but contribute to the success of the core telecommunications network.

The successful Universal Card has made AT&T the second-largest credit card issuer in the United States after Citicorp. When a survey discovered that only 19 percent of AT&Ts employees thought top management's statements were believable, the company magazine printed it. Now high executives have rated their bosses and been rated in turn, and this upward feedback is spreading throughout the company.[4]

Compared with some newer firms, AT&T has, at times, seemed more than a little clumsy. Weighted down with employees and unaccustomed to the thrust and parry of the open marketplace, the company reported disappointing earnings in the first several postdivestiture years. AT&T demonstrated its marketing naïveté when it made a ballyhooed entry into the personal computer business. The company assigned its old-line sales force, used to dealing with captive customers, to handle unfamiliar high-tech products and grapple with entrenched competitors. The result was losses of around $3 billion. A modest turnaround began in 1986. AT&T has cut over $1 billion through employee reductions and plant modernization.[5]

RESTRUCTURING THE IBM SALES FORCE

The late 1980s and early 1990s saw major changes for IBM. Their competition was specializing and eating away at technology niches. Customers were looking for more specialized sales support, and IBM primarily provided generalist skills. In addition, customers wanted highly responsive vendors at a time when IBM was slow to move due to their large bureaucracy.

During this period, IBM was structured by geography, using local teams assigned to customer accounts. These teams were highly dependent on the marketing support teams located at an area's central location. Whenever a bid was sought by a customer, the local team had to go through many layers of staff for approval for any special bids or special systems requirements, which could take a few weeks. This inability to respond quickly caused dissatisfaction among customers.

IBM's Sales Structure

To improve its responsiveness and quality of support, IBM made many changes that capitalized on the size of the organization and its greatest resource, its customers and employees. Customer responsiveness was improved by giving salespeople greater authority and by retraining the sales force as specialists.

Customers were frustrated with IBM's high prices because they felt that IBM's competition offered comparable, more affordable products. This lead to the major restructuring of IBM in the early 1990s in which the corporation reduced their staff levels from a high of 400,000 to 225,000 in 1994.

IBM was able to reduce costs by removing the various marketing support layers. Frequently, these individuals were managers in training and did not have the skills required to support the field. They were used primarily as liaisons to the development or engineering workforce. By reducing this layer and giving the sales force a more direct route to the development groups, IBM has reduced the response time for customer inquiries, and this has allowed the development group to be more in tune with customers' needs.

IBM was forced to reduce its product cost structure due to shrinking competitive advantage and differentiation in its product lines. It reduced costs by removing the support team costs from the product and having the customer pay separately for support services. This change, however, caused problems with those customers who did value their support.

The restructuring efforts forced IBM to look at the sales force skill base and develop a strategy that would protect its core competencies and deliver a competitive advantage. Static competitive advantage is no longer realistic. The dynamic changes that the technology industry is experiencing demand flexibility from a company to remain competitive. To meet these changes, IBM has focused on its core skills, for which specialized individuals are constantly being trained. Many general skills were viewed as being nonstrategic and became outsourced to business partners.

IBM has developed a new sales method for account coverage. It has developed industry verticals whereby salespeople are trained to understand a specific industry and to provide particular solutions to these IBM customers. The territory sales areas, based on location, were eliminated and account coverage was handled through the industry verticals. The following material outlines the steps in providing account coverage.

Accounts are now handled by the industry sales representative who is responsible for the ongoing efforts with the customer and for overall customer satisfaction. When a customer need arises, the salesperson will bring in the appropriate systems specialists to assist in addressing the solution. The team selling concept allows IBM to match their expert with the customer's expert. For example, a salesperson who knows store systems and point-of-sale (POS) devices will work with the customer's store systems group, while an IBM communications specialist works with the customer's communication group. This type of approach has allowed IBM to provide better service to their customers through greater industry and technical knowledge.

As a means to get the sales force more focused on customer needs, IBM has begun to regularly monitor customer satisfaction levels. All of IBM's sales force, administration, and headquarters personnel are evaluated and compensated based on customer satisfaction. IBM believes that its customer relationships, developed over the past fifty years, are its most important resource and that these relationships must be protected.

Another step that IBM took to reduce costs is the shift to a mobile workforce. The introduction of a mobile workforce and the development of industry verticals were both significant changes for the sales force. Salespeople could no longer get together with their management or peers on a regular basis to strategize, they did not have administrative support available to them to assist with daily tasks, and they no longer had the convenience or comfort of having their own cubicle. To successfully make this change, IBM had to provide the sales force with the proper tools.

All sales support individuals were given a notebook PC with a modem and PC software to support their sales efforts. The software packages included a word processor, a spreadsheet, a presentation package, fax capabilities, daily planners with a directory, software update utilities, and a package to tie into IBM's mainframe systems, such as e-mail and product and customer information. These systems provided the sales force with the tools required to accomplish their customer support goals. Since the move to these systems was quite radical for IBM, it spent a great deal on training to assist the sales force.

IBM has also developed a new opportunity analysis software package to support the sales force in its new work environment. This system was designed to manage and improve account coverage by optimizing resources. Due to the reduction of the sales force, the salespeople now have larger territories and more customers. The opportunity analysis software was designed to assist the sales manager in prioritizing opportunities and allocating the proper resources to an opportunity.

The modified sales process works in this manner. Someone in IBM will be contacted about a customer opportunity. This person could be anyone in the organization. Based on the type of customer opportunity, it will be forwarded to the appropriate manager. This manager will either assign the customer opportunity to a salesperson or designate a business partner. If IBM does not offer a solution for this problem, the customer will be notified. Once the customer is contacted, the system will be updated to acknowledge the request. This step improves customer service by providing a response to all customer requests. It also ensures that IBM is maximizing all of its customer opportunities by using a tracking system. Once the customer is contacted, relevant information about the customer opportunity, such as revenue potential, skills required, and time frame, will be recorded in the system. A customer opportunity owner will be assigned to the account, and this person becomes responsible for updating the system on any changes throughout the sales process.

This system offers many benefits to IBM, including improved customer service and improved resource optimization. One of the drawbacks is that the system is only as good as the inputted information. Despite this drawback, the system is viewed as a tool for better customer service. The ultimate measure of the success of the new sales process is having a system that maximizes IBM's profitability and addresses the customers' needs to their complete satisfaction.

The layoffs caused by IBM's restructuring created morale concerns. IBM has addressed these issues by investing heavily in sales force training. All sales support individuals go through three week-long training sessions. These classes focus on empowerment, territory management, time management, and PC training. The flattening of the sales force infrastructure has also reduced the number of growth opportunities for the salespeople.

One of IBM's strengths in the past was the large size of its sales force. Many customers felt secure in knowing that IBM always had someone available to assist them. However, the cost of this service reduced IBM's price competitiveness. IBM was required to remove this support layer so that its price structure could remain competitive.

HEWLETT-PACKARD AND REENGINEERING

The Hewlett-Packard's (HP) Telecommunications Sales Organization has recently decided to reorganize its sales districts in an effort to target two large telephone companies. A fourth sales district was formed to generate sales of specialized telecommunications equipment to these two large telephone companies. Hewlett-Packard has been successful in selling these specialized products to the rest of the telephone companies.

The market potential for specialized telecommunications equipment for each telephone company was determined to be $100 million a year. Based on sales to other telephone companies of similar size, HP's sales potential to each telephone company is 20 percent of the market potential, or about $20 million a year.

HP has never been strong in selling products to the telecommunications services industry, especially the telephone companies. Any sales previously made to telephone companies were limited to their management information systems departments.

Recently, HP has built several applications for the telecommunications industry, specifically targeting the telephone companies. One such application is the HP Video Server. The Video Server is a component for the Video Dial Tone services that the telephone companies are trying to launch in order to compete against cable TV companies. It is capable of storing thousands of video movie titles and transmitting them simultaneously to hundreds of homes. This application costs in the range of $3 million to $15 million, depending on the configuration of the system. The sales cycle to sell this system typically takes one to three years. HP has been successful in selling this product to the other telephone companies.

Once accounts managers have been brought on board, they need to go through the HP orientation process. Although there is a significant time pressure to get new salespeople to generate enough revenue to meet the three-year sales objective, HP has lost new salespeople, especially from small companies that became overwhelmed with their size and bureaucracy. The new salespeople also needed to be trained on HP products, but not in as much detail as the product specialists.

HP has recently issued notebook PCs to most of its sales force. These tools have improved productivity tremendously when large systems, such as video servers and data collection systems, are sold. It has helped in customizing sales presentations and creating sales proposals. However, HP still has not yet implemented a groupware application such as Lotus Notes.

Team selling requires coordination and communication among the members of the team. It is imperative to understand what each team member is doing in the account. The team needs to have a common database of customer lists and associated activities. When generating a proposal, various people, including the factory engineers, need to verify proposal information. Quotation of a system usually requires several layers of management sign-offs. Various commitments need to be documented. A groupware application such as Lotus Notes will be able to address all these issues and more. Such an application, if implemented well, will increase the speed and flexibility, as well as the accountability, of a large system team-selling effort and give HP a competitive advantage.[6]

HEALTH CARE AND REENGINEERING

The health care field has also embraced reengineering. (See Figure 8.1 for an evaluation of servicing time as related to reengineering.) As hospitals are frantically cutting costs to survive in this environment, they have also begun to cut their biggest single expense—nursing. Recently, during a severe nursing shortage, jobs were plentiful, signing bonuses were common, and union contracts were doubling nurses' salaries at many hospitals to more than $50,000 in just two years. Shorter hospital stays and discounted hospital rates demanded by managed care companies are placing a strain on hospi-

FIGURE 8.1. Hospital Performance Efficiency Based on Servicing Time to Determine the Need for a Reengineering Effort

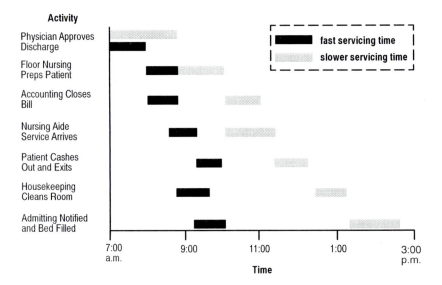

tal budgets. Hospitals that once fought one another to attract nurses now see their large nursing staffs as burdens and have begun to lay off nurses.

Acute care facilities are cross-training nonprofessionals to do bed baths, feed patients, perform EKGs, draw blood, and take vital signs. They are combining and eliminating programs and departments in an effort to streamline processes and save money. These dramatic changes have resulted in the downsizing of large numbers of professional nursing positions, which has resulted in layoffs.

The literature supports that negative feelings toward changes are common place. Managed care and reengineering resulted in many unsettling changes. Professional nurses are facing a loss of self-identity, increased risk of alienation, and confusion. Change makes things different, and this normally can lead to negativity. Whenever possible, it is always preferable to plan change. When the effects of change are intentional and taken into account, it may be possible to decrease the negative feelings toward these changes. Negative feelings lead to resistance to change, which depends on human characteristics such as personalities, perceptions, and personal need. Resistance to change is always found when the change one is experiencing is forced.

Though nurses have always been the change agents in health care, nursing is not prepared for this type of constant state of change, and many believed that they would always have a job. They believed that their benefits would increase over time, their schedule would improve with increased seniority, and, if they wanted it, overtime would always be available. The changes in the health care system have changed all of this. No one is sure what will happen next. There is not even confidence that the leadership is sure where it is going or can predict the next move.

Downsizing has nurses worried and stressed about the future of nursing and job security. The literature very clearly describes the resistance people have to change. Causes of resistance to change include parochial self-interest, which will result in political behavior, misunderstanding, and lack of trust; different assessments, which can lead to differences in analyses; low tolerance for change, that is, intellectually understanding but emotionally not accepting; and resistance as a reaction to change agent's attitude.

A connection exists between resistance to change and increased stress and illness caused by stress. Nurses are normally under higher levels of stress, and the current environment is making matters worse. Furthermore, it has been found that rates of depression in nurses are higher than in the general population. Stress-related diseases, including hypertension, are five times higher in nurses, ulcers are ten times higher in nurses, and nearly one in four surveyed nurses say they often have difficulty falling asleep, as compared to one in eleven workers nationally. Nurses also experience a higher incidence of chronic fatigue, cardiovascular disease, and mental illness as stress increases.

Nurses require assistance through the entire change process caused by reengineering and downsizing to ensure everyone, staff and management, are successful. A communication process that will assist the nurses to successfully implement the necessary changes is needed. To implement change successfully, there must be communication. A transformation framework that can be used offers eight steps leadership can utilize to implement the change process by outlining the communication method. The first step is to establish a sense of urgency. The CEO or Director of Nursing must outline the importance of the change and the outcomes that must be achieved. This establishes the source of the information formally to everyone so that everyone is clear. Second, a powerful coalition of all levels in the hospital is developed. This coalition conducts the third step of creating the vision—How will the changes occur? What will the changes involve?—This team is one of quality. It will have the knowledge and data for planning, implementing, evaluating, and problem solving. This coalition will have the power to ensure the realization of the vision. The fourth step is communicating the vision. Meetings are held at all unit and service levels to communicate the changes, the vision, to all staff. These meetings will happen as often as needed.

The members of the coalition must be the communication ambassadors. They must make sure that what is going to happen is understood. They also must be positive about the decisions made and communicate that as well. They must not filter or manipulate information. The fifth step is to empower others to act on the vision. The coalition should be identifying any obstacles to reduce staff anxiety and to increase participation in the changes that have occurred. It is at this point that the major changes have occurred in the hospital or health care agency. The next step is planning for short-term wins. The staff directly involved with the work give input on the changes and simple changes are discussed. At the seventh step, the simple changes are consolidated into still more changes. The vision has been implemented with new projects being identified. The eighth step is an ongoing exploration of ways to streamline major systems.

This framework allows for decisions to occur quickly, while informing the staff of what is occurring—an important concept in reengineering. It empowers people to act, and once people are empowered, some major obstacles toward change are removed.

PENNSYLVANIA STATE EMPLOYEES CREDIT UNION

When 297 of Pennsylvania State Employees Credit Union employees went on strike from July 8 to October 8, 1997, the result was a reengineering of positions and work that enabled the credit union to survive the crisis. Before the strike, twenty-nine loan officers answered member calls, entered the information into Fair Isaac's Credit Desk system, pulled a credit report, made a decision, and responded to the member. All of this took an average of fifteen minutes. As a result, 25 percent of members waiting in the queue abandoned the calls. During the strike, ten temporary workers answered calls and entered information into Credit Desk. They told members the credit union would call back. After pulling the credit report, the loan went to one of five management decision makers, who reviewed the application and credit report, made a decision, and returned the member's call. After reengineering, members were on the phone, on average, only three to five minutes. Reengineering increased the number of calls answered by 25 percent. The additional calls resulted in increased loan volume despite decreased staffing.[7]

PERSONAL RESTRUCTURING

Reengineering relates not just to a radical redesign of business processes in organizations, but also to individuals in the organization. To properly reengineer, it is important to have a job description and to assess the actual job skills based on that job description:

- Determine whether any professional training is needed for management, interpersonal, or computer skills.
- Stay aware of the general work flow of any adjoining divisions.
- Attend industry informational seminars and trade shows.
- Make positive business connections with external professionals.
- Keep an updated résumé.
- Set a career path.
- Assist in the restructuring process.
- Keep a positive self-image by being confident.[8]

What Americans do on the job will change. The old blue-collar elite will give way to an ascendant class, technical workers who program computers or conduct laboratory tests or fix copiers. Almost everyone, up through the highest ranks of professionals, will feel increased pressure to specialize or, at least, to package himself or herself as a marketable portfolio of skills.[9]

To achieve megachanges, it is important to set goals that may seem unattainable, motivate people to reach those goals, and give them the resources to do so. It is essential to set goals, monitor progress, and provide feedback throughout any period of restructuring. It is also important to be able to quantify results in the end.[10] Responding to the competitive dynamic created by information technology, many large companies have drastically downsized, divested, and outsourced to reduce the costs and complexity of their operations. Yet, simply reducing the size of a corporation is not the solution.

Many companies have spent decades automating pieces of their businesses, scattering networks and incompatible computer platforms throughout their organizations. However, the empowered, decentralized teams of the information economy need a unified view of what is happening within an organization. Coherent behavior must be governed by an enterprise model that codifies the corporation's intent and "how we do things around here." A coherent model should include "how we change how we do things around here." Adding the institutional ability to adapt in a dynamic environment has become a survival imperative for most companies.[11]

In an "age of reengineering," an individual will necessarily keep himself or herself more market ready—constantly scanning to identify the market for his or her services, and honing those distinctive services so that they continue to have value in that market.

INTEGRATION MANAGEMENT

The tendency to see integration as a unique event in an organization's life is magnified by the fact that acquisitions and mergers often are painful and anxiety-producing experiences. They involve job loss, restructured responsibilities, derailed careers, and diminished power.

Industry consolidations, the globalization of competition, technological developments, and other trends have touched off an unprecedented wave of mergers and acquisitions that shows no signs of abating. According to figures from the Securities Data Company, the dollar value of U.S. mergers and acquisitions announced in 1996 alone grew more than 27 percent, to $658.8 billion from $518 billion in 1995. Despite this enormous growth in merger activity, acquisitions that appear to be both financially and strategically sound on paper often turn out to be disappointing for many companies.

A study reported in the *Economist* of 300 major mergers conducted over a ten-year period found that in 57 percent of these merged companies, return to shareholders lagged behind the average for their industries. The faster people from both companies are given opportunities to work together on important business issues, the faster integration will occur.[12]

In a survey of 580 organizations worldwide from four industries—computers, autos, hospitals, and banks—the American Quality Foundation and Ernst & Young found that 31 percent of the U.S. enterprises regularly benchmarked their products and services. The first step in benchmarking is to understand your own process in detail.[13]

To get ahead of the competition and help buyers get ahead of theirs, stay on the lookout for new and better ways of doing business. Make a company known as a forward-thinking organization that is willing and able to adapt to rapid changes in business and technology. Information is vital to innovation—read business and industry publications regularly and stay alert to changes in other industries that might affect yours. Check out a competitor's Web page to find out what they are up to and what effect their activities and plans will have on your business.[14]

The best value-added feature is a firm commitment to meet customer needs and improve performance. It is not only what a company sells that counts, but how a product or service is sold that makes the difference between success and failure. Value-added selling shifts the focus of business relationships from price to all the other more important reasons why your customers should take their business to your company.[15]

CONCLUSION

Companies wishing to undertake reengineering must learn some lessons and then apply them. First, it is important to set realistic expectations for reengineering. Companies whose management understood reengineering achieved the best results. Next, aim high when setting targets. Although actual results tend to underperform expected results, aiming for high targets induces greater motivation on the part of those involved with the initiative, yielding better results. Also, be selective in choosing what to reengineer. Goals and performance measurements will not yield the desired results unless they are applied to strategic areas of a company. Processes should be examined for their strategic impact as candidates for reengineering.

Evidence mounts that the accompanying shift in paradigms, from business as making things to business as providing a service, is under way. More and more work will be done by teams addressing projects that have a beginning and an end. Smart companies are using reengineering to solve their toughest problems. There will be fewer managers, and employees cannot count on spending thirty years with the same employer.

Employees in competitive organizations will need to be more multifunctional, which will mean having effective communication and interpersonal skills in the organization and with customers, as well as good technology skills and self-management skills in performing their own tasks. Managers will need to be highly proficient in using management strategies and should constantly retool and reeducate themselves to stay current with these principles. Reengineering also shows that managers need to be more humanistic in managing people to maximize their productivity, despite having limited resources and "doing more with less." In addition, managers must also be much more astute to complex changes in the marketplace and help their organizations adapt so that they can take advantage of new opportunities.

Effective Reengineering

- Develop clear measurable goals.
- Get customers involved in the reengineering process.
- Have a level of "buy in" with input from all employees.
- Try to accomplish early successes.
- Maintain senior-level management commitment.
- Focus on macro strategic changes in the organization.
- Create an action-oriented environment.

CASE STUDY

Bentex Corporation

Synopsis

Bentex's goal is to keep account executives focused on attaining their sales and customer service objectives while it is going through a merger and reorganization and significant downsizing.

Background

Bentex Corporation sells telecommunications products internationally, with a major focus on the northeastern section of the United States (New York and New England). Linda Giordano's division sells to the largest accounts only via nine branches—six in New York and three in New England. She is the Branch Manager responsible for the Long Island Branch and the private health care and private education accounts in New York City.

Key Goal

Keep the sales force focused.

Description of Problem/Issue

Sales objectives have increased by 20 percent despite a number of factors that have distracted Linda's sales force. In addition, Bentex is facing increased competition from existing and new companies.

Various distractions (such as merger, reorganization, downsizing) have many at Bentex wondering what the impact will be on their jobs. With such huge objectives and new competitors challenging them, Linda and her management team need to keep the salespeople focused and motivated.

Alternate Solutions

To date, Linda has increased communications to her team, keeping them current on all situations, and they have introduced a branch recognition program to highlight significant contributions toward the attainment of sales and servicing objectives.

Input

Linda has come to you knowing that, as a fellow manager, you have experienced a similar situation and wants to know how you handled it successfully. What would you advise Linda to do?

Notes

Chapter 1

1. T. Carter, *Contemporary Sales Force Management,* Binghamton, NY: The Haworth Press, Inc., 1998.

2. S. Frank, "Chase May Cut Up to About 3000 Positions," *The Wall Street Journal* (February 6, 1998), p. A3.

3. W. Bulkeley and M. Maremont, "Kodak's 10,000 Job Cuts May Really Amount to Just 8,000 at End of Day," *The Wall Street Journal* (November 13, 1997), p. A4.

4. R. Narisetti, "IBM Lays off Staff in North American Sales, Distribution," *The Wall Street Journal* (November 17, 1997), p. B16.

5. D. Khalish, "IBM, Dell in $16 Billion Pact," *Press & Sun-Bulletin* (March 5, 1999), p. B10.

6. R. Narisetti, "J. P. Morgan Lays off 100 People in Asia in Cost-Cutting Plan," *The Wall Street Journal* (March 2, 1998), p. B3.

7. J. Auerbach, "Digital Equipment Exceeds Estimates Earning $306.8 Million After a Gain," *The Wall Street Journal* (April 17, 1998), p. B10.

8. G. Hamel, "Will Merger with DEC Be Compaq's Last Hurrah?", *The Wall Street Journal* (March 2, 1998), p. A18.

9. R. Simison and F. Warner, "Motown Greets Merger Plans As Good News," *The Wall Street Journal* (May 7, 1998), p. B1.

10. M. Murray, "Bankers Trust Mulls Restructuring of Asian Operation Amid Crisis," *The Wall Street Journal* (February 5, 1998), p. B4.

11. C. Goldsmith, "Reengineering After Trailing Boeing for Years, Airbus Aims for 50% of the Market," *The Wall Street Journal* (March 16, 1998), p. A1.

12. H. Lancaster, "Data General Expects $125 Million Charge for Restructuring," *The Wall Street Journal* (June 2, 1998), p. A4.

13. D. Ball, "Alitalia Shows Signs of Turnaround After Years of Ills," *The Wall Street Journal* (December 31, 1997), p. B4.

14. Q. Hardy, "Motorola Posts Profit Below Forecasts," *The Wall Street Journal* (January 13, 1998), p. A3.

15. D. Clark and G. C. Hill, "Motorola Plans to Slash Staff, Take a Charge," *The Wall Street Journal* (June 5, 1998), p. A3.

16. V. O'Connell, "Nabisco to Take $406 Million Charge, Cut 6% of Work Force in Retrenchment," *The Wall Street Journal* (June 9, 1998), p. A4.

17. R. Narisetti, "Xerox to Cut 9,000 Jobs Over Two Years," *The Wall Street Journal* (April 8, 1998), p. A3.

18. M. Brannigan and James Hagerty, "Sunbeam Plans to Cut 5,100 Jobs As CEO Promises Rebound from Dismal Quarter," *The Wall Street Journal* (May 12, 1998), p. A3.

19. E. Jensen, "GTE Corp. Unveils Major Restructuring," *The Wall Street Journal* (April 3, 1998), p. A3.

20. R. Gibson, "General Mills Gets in Shape for Turnaround," *The Wall Street Journal* (October 25, 1995), p. B3.

21. T. Carter, "Sales and Marketing Management and Reengineering," *International Association of Management Proceedings,* Montreal, Canada, Vol. 15, No. 1, 1997, pp. 139-145.

22. T. Stewart, "Welcome to the Revolution," *Fortune* (December 13, 1993), pp. 67-77.

23. S. Sherman, "How Will We Live with the Tumult?", *Fortune* (December 13, 1993), pp. 123-125.

24. J. Duck, "Managing Change: The Art of Balancing," *Harvard Business Review,* Vol. 71, No. 6, November/December 1993, p. 109.

25. W. Kiechel, "A Manager's Career in the New Economy," *Fortune* (April 4, 1994), p. 68.

26. L. Richman, "Managing Through a Downturn," *Fortune* (August, 1995), p. 59.

27. L. Qingyun, Personal Interview, Beijing University, China, June 2, 1997.

28. M. Magnet, "Let's Go for Growth," *Fortune* (March 7, 1994), p. 61.

29. R. Norton, "Job Destruction/Job Creation," *Fortune* (April 1, 1996), p. 5.

Chapter 2

1. W. Keenan, "Death of the Sales Manager," *Sales & Marketing Management Magazine* (October 1994), p. 67.

2. B. Fox, "Reengineering Revisited," *Chain Store Age Executive,* Vol. 71, No. 3. March 1995, p. 176.

3. J. Ross, "Does Shuffling the Deck Work?" *Harvard Business Review,* Vol. 75, No. 6, November/December 1997, p. 17.

4. A. Cohen, "Facing Pressure," *Sales & Marketing Management Magazine* (April 1997), p. 30.

5. J. Lawlor, "Aaargh Burnout," *Sales & Marketing Management Magazine* (March 1997), p. 46.

6. R. Henkoff, "Getting Beyond Downsizing," *Fortune* (January 10, 1994), p. 58.

7. B. Dumaine, "Tough Bosses," *Fortune* (October 18, 1993), p. 39.

8. A. Fisher, "Welcome to the Age of Overwork," *Fortune* (November 30, 1992), p. 64.

9. H. Levinson, "Burn Out," *Harvard Business Review,* Vol. 74, No. 4, July/August 1996, p. 153.

10. A. Fisher, "The Downside of Downsizing," *Fortune* (May 23, 1988), p. 42.

11. J. Spiers, "Upper Middle-Class Woes," *Fortune* (December 27, 1993), p. 82.

12. J. Fierman, "When Will You Get a Raise?" *Fortune* (July 12, 1993), p. 34.

13. B. Wysocki, "Retaining Employees," *The Wall Street Journal* (September 8, 1997), p. A1.

14. K. Labich, "The New Unemployed," *Fortune* (March 8, 1993), p. 40.

15. M. Zinn, "The Aftermath of Corporate Re-Engineering," *Credit World*, Vol. 86, No. 2, November/December 1997, p. 35.

16. L. Richman, "When Will the Layoffs End?" *Fortune* (March 8, 1993), p. 54.

17. H. Lancaster, "Will Hiring a Full Staff Be the Next Fashion in Management?" *The Wall Street Journal* (April 28, 1998), p. B1.

18. S. Shellenbarger, "Some Employers Find Way to Ease Burdens of Changing Shifts," *The Wall Street Journal* (March 25, 1998), p. B1.

19. P. Drucker, *Managing for the Future, the 1990s and Beyond,* New York: Dutton, 1992.

20. B. O'Reilly, "Your New Global Work Force," *Fortune* (December 14, 1992), p. 52.

Chapter 3

1. K. Labich, "Making Over Middle Managers," *Fortune* (May 8, 1989), p. 58.

2. K. Sissell, "Reexamining Reengineering: Down to Microsurgery," *Chemical Week*, Vol. 158, No. 22, June 5, 1996, p. 29.

3. T. Carter, "Sales and Marketing Management and Reengineering," *International Association of Management Proceedings, Montreal, Canada,* Vol. 15, No. 1, 1997, pp. 139-145.

4. T. Stewart, "Do You Push Your People Too Hard?" *Fortune* (October 22, 1990), p. 121.

5. T. Carter, "Sales and Marketing Management and Reengineering," *International Association of Management Proceedings, Montreal, Canada,* Vol. 15, No. 1, 1997, pp. 139-145.

6. J. Moore, "Predators and Prey: A New Ecology of Competition," *Harvard Business Week*, Vol. 71, No. 3, May/June, 1993, p. 75.

7. W. Keenan, "Caught in a Vicious Cycle," *Sales & Marketing Management Magazine* (January 1997), p. 49.

8. A. Perkins, "The Costs of Inflexible Job Arrangements," *Harvard Business Review,* Vol. 71, No. 4, July/August 1993, p. 9.

9. S. Brown and K. Eisenhardt, "Time Pacing: Competing in Markets That Won't Stand Still," *Harvard Business Review,* Vol. 76, No. 2, March/April 1998, p. 59.

10. J. Brower and T. Hout, "Fast Cycle Capability for Competitive Power," *Harvard Business Review*, Vol. 66, No. 6, November/December 1988, p. 110.

11. B. Dumaine, "How Managers Can Succeed Through Speed," *Fortune* (February 13, 1989), p. 54.

12. G. Stalk, "Time—The Next Source of Competitive Advantage," *Harvard Business Review,* Vol. 66, No. 4, July/August 1988, p. 44.

13. C. Berning, J. Jacoby, and G. Szybillo, "Time and Consumer Behavior: An Interdisciplinary Overview," *Journal of Consumer Research,* Vol. 2, March 1976, p. 320.

14. R. King, "Levi's Factory Workers Are Assigned to Teams and Morale Takes a Hit," *The Wall Street Journal* (May 20, 1998), p. A1.

15. J. Barsoux and J. Manzoni, "The Set Up to Fail Syndrome," *Harvard Business Review,* Vol. 76, No. 2, March/April 1998, p. 101.

Chapter 4

1. F. Gouillart and F. Sturdivant, "Spend a Day in the Life of Your Customers," *Harvard Business Review,* Vol. 72, No. 1, January/February 1994, p. 116.

2. L. Kellaway, "Getting the Flavour of the Business," *Financial Times* (April 27, 1998), p. 11.

3. K. Blanchard, "Get the Power," *Selling Power* (April 1998), p. 44.

4. T. Carter, *Contemporary Sales Force Management,* Binghamton, NY: The Haworth Press, Inc., 1998.

5. T. Kiely, "Reengineering: It Doesn't Have to Be All or Nothing," *Harvard Business Review,* Vol. 73, No. 6, November/December 1995, p. 16.

6. G. Brewer, "Brain Power," *Sales & Marketing Management Magazine* (May 1997), p. 39.

7. J. Bessen, "Riding the Marketing Information Wave," *Harvard Business Review,* Vol. 71, No. 5, September/October 1993, p. 150.

8. R. Jacob, "Beyond Quality and Value," *Fortune* (Autumn/Winter 1993), p. 8.

9. D. Dunn and C. Thomas, "Reengineering Marketing," *Review of Business* (Spring 1996), p. 41.

10. J. Hyatt, "Hot Commodity," *Inc.* (February 1996), p. 50.

11. M. Campanelli, "Reshuffling the Deck," *Sales & Marketing Management Magazine* (June 1994), p. 83.

12. W. Keenan, "Plugging into Your Customer's Needs," *Sales & Marketing Management Magazine* (January 1996), p. 62.

13. G. Brewer, "Love the Ones You're With," *Sales & Marketing Management Magazine* (May 1996), p. 38.

14. R. Whiteley, "Are You Driven to Action?" *Sales & Marketing Management Magazine* (June 1994), p. 31.

15. R. Blattberg and J. Deighton, "Manage Marketing by the Customer Equity Test," *Harvard Business Review,* Vol. 74, No. 4, July/August 1996, p. 136.

16. K. Coyne and R. Dye, "The Competitive Dynamics of Network Based Business," *Harvard Business Review,* Vol. 76, No. 1, January/February 1998, p. 99.

17. T. Morrison, "Meet the New Consumer," *Fortune* (Autumn/Winter 1993), p. 6.

18. E. Rasmusson, "Winning Back Angry Customers," *Sales & Marketing Management Magazine* (October 1997), p. 131.

Chapter 5

1. D. Jones and R. Recardo, "A Report Card on Reengineering," *Production and Inventory Management Journal,* Vol. 38, No. 3, Third Quarter 1997, p. 51.

2. R. Kaplan and D. Norton, "The Balanced Scorecard—Measures That Drive Performance," *Harvard Business Review* Vol. 70, No. 1, January/February 1992), p. 68.

3. R. Kaplan and D. Norton, "Putting the Balanced Scorecard to Work," *Harvard Business Review,* Vol. 71, No. 5, September/October 1993, p. 79.

4. R. Kaplan and D. Norton, "Using the Balanced Scorecard As a Strategic Management System," *Harvard Business Review,* Vol. 74, No. 1, January/February 1996, p. 92.

5. M. Boone, "Staying in Front of Your Reps-Virtually," *Sales & Marketing Management Magazine* (April 1997), p. 32.

6. A. McAfee and D. Upton, "The Real Virtual Factory," *Harvard Business Review,* Vol. 74, No. 4, July/August 1996, p. 123.

7. D. C , "Trust in Virtual Teams," *Harvard Business Review,* Vol. 76, No. 3, May/June 1998, p. 20.

8. N. Alster, "What Flexible Workers Can Do," *Fortune* (February 12, 1989), p. 62.

9. W. Pape, "Remote Control," *Inc. Technology,* Vol. 18, No. 13, September 17, 1996, p. 25.

10. M. Murray, "Chase Manhattan Hopes to Expand Using Technology," *The Wall Street Journal* (May 27, 1998), p. B4.

11. J. Kim, "Virtual 'Net' Banks Offer Real Savings," *The Wall Street Journal* (May 15, 1998), p. B7.

12. S. Goldman, R. Nagel, and K. Preiss, *Agile Competitors and Virtual Organizations,* New York: Van Nostrand Reinhold, 1995.

13. R. Ackoff, *The Democratic Corporation,* New York: Oxford, 1994.

14. T. Kily, "Business Processes: Consider Outsourcing," *Harvard Business Review,* Vol. 75, No. 3, May/June 1997, p. 11.

15. T. Carter, *Contemporary Sales Force Management,* Binghamton, NY: The Haworth Press, Inc., 1998.

16. S. Sherman, "The New Computer Revolution," *Fortune* (June 14, 1993), p. 57.

17. N. Arnott, "Getting with the Program," *Performance* (March, 1995), p. 39.

18. T. Davenport, "Saving It's Soul: Human Centered Information Management," *Harvard Business Review,* Vol. 72, No. 2, March/April 1994, p. 119.

19. K. Starr, "Transforming Sales," *Selling Power* (January/February 1998), p. 30.

20. S. Ghosh, "Making Business Sense of the Internet," *Harvard Business Review,* Vol. 76, No. 2, March/April 1998, p. 126.

21. M. Adams, "Messages," *Sales & Marketing Management Magazine* (June 1997), p. 73.

22. E. Rasmusson, "Setting Your Sights on Videoconferencing," *Sales & Marketing Management Magazine* (September 1997), p. 106.

23. J. Yarbrough, "Salvaging a Lousy Year," *Sales & Marketing Management Magazine* (July 1996), p. 70.

24. S. Goldman, R. Nagel, and K. Preiss, *Cooperate to Compete*, New York: Van Nostrand Reinhold, 1996.

25. C. Baldwin and K. Clark, "Managing in an Age of Modularity," *Harvard Business Review,* Vol. 75, No. 5, September/October 1997, p. 84.

26. L. Greiner, "Evolution and Revolution As Organizations Grow," *Harvard Business Review,* Vol. 76, No. 3, May/June 1998, p. 55.

27. L. Gioja, M. Millemann, and R. Pascale, "Changing the Way We Change," *Harvard Business Review,* Vol. 75, No. 5, November/December 1997, p. 127.

28. H. Courtney, J. Kirkland, and P. Viquerie, "Strategy Under Uncertainty," *Harvard Business Review,* Vol. 75, No. 6, November/December 1997, p. 67.

29. B. Sells, "What Asbestos Taught Me About Managing Risk," *Harvard Business Review,* Vol. 72, No. 2, March/April 1994, p. 76.

30. D. Light, "Avoiding the Crisis You Don't Want to Manage," *Harvard Business Review,* Vol. 75, No. 5, September/October 1997, p. 10.

31. L. Paine, "Managing for Organizational Integrity," *Harvard Business Review,* Vol. 72, No. 2, March/April 1994, p. 106.

32. B. Dumaine, "Times Are Good? Create a Crisis," *Fortune* (June 28, 1993), p. 123.

33. B. Walsh, "Beware the Crisis Lovers," *Forbes Asap* (June 5, 1995), p. 17.

34. J. Conger, D. Finegold, and E. Lawler, "Appraising Board Room Performance," *Harvard Business Review,* Vol. 76, No. 1, January/February 1998, p. 136.

35. T. Stewart, "The King Is Dead," *Fortune* (January 11, 1993), p. 34.

36. T. Carter, "Sounding Board," *Selling Power* (May 1999), p. 44.

37. S. Sherman, "How Tomorrow's Best Leaders Are Learning Their Stuff," *Fortune* (November 27, 1995), p. 91.

38. S. Goldman, R. Nagel, and K. Preiss, *Agile Competitors and Virtual Organizations,* New York: Van Nostrand Reinhold, 1995.

Chapter 6

1. R. Wellins, "Making Reengineering Human," *Journal of Services Marketing,* Vol. 9, No. 3, 1995, p. 51.

2. R. Frey, "Empowerment or Else," *Harvard Business Review,* Vol. 71, No. 5, September/October 1993, p. 80.

3. G. Hall, J. Rosenthal, and Judy Wade, "How to Make Reengineering Really Work," *Harvard Business Review,* Vol. 71, No. 6, November/December 1993, p. 119.

4. K. Dowd and J. Liedtka, "What Corporations Seek in MBA Hires: A Survey," *Selections,* Vol. 10, No. 2, Winter 1994, p. 36.

5. G. Benson, "On the Campus: How Well Do Business Schools Prepare Graduates for the Business World?" *Personnel* (July/August, 1983), p. 61.

6. L. Branch, "Poll Shows Firms Give Hiring Priority to Communicating, Job Experience," *The Star-Ledger* (October 28, 1991), p. 9.

7. B. Smith, "Process Reengineering: The Toughest Challenge," *H. R. Focus,* Vol. 72, No. 2, February 1995, p. 24.

:

8. C. Argyris, "Empowerment: The Emperor's New Clothes," *Harvard Business Review,* Vol. 76, No. 3, May/June 1998, p. 98.

9. A. Farnham, "The Trust Gap," *Fortune* (December 4, 1989), p. 56.

10. W. Kiechel, "How Important Is Morale, Really?" *Fortune* (February 13, 1989), p. 121.

11. L. Smith, "The Executive's New Coach," *Fortune* (December 27, 1993), p. 126.

12. D. Leonard and S. Straus, "Putting Your Company's Whole Brain to Work," *Harvard Business Review,* Vol. 75, No. 4, July/August 1997, p. 111.

13. R. Goffee and G. Jones, "What Holds the Modern Company Together?" *Harvard Business Review,* Vol. 74, No. 6, November/December 1996, p. 133.

14. L. Bourgeois, K. Eisenhardt, and J. Kahwajy, "How Management Teams Can Have a Good Fight," *Harvard Business Review,* Vol. 75, No. 4, July/August 1997, p. 77.

15. B. Dumaine, "Who Needs a Boss?" *Fortune* (May 7, 1990), p. 52.

16. S. Caminiti, "What Team Leaders Need to Know," *Fortune* (February 20, 1995), p. 93.

17. M. Marchetti, "Why Teams Fail?" *Sales & Marketing Management Magazine* (June, 1997), p. 91.

18. D. Barton and T. Hsieh, "Young Lions, High Priests and Old Warriors," *The McKinsey Quarterly,* No. 2, 1995, p. 62.

19. J. Huey, "The New Post-Heroic Leadership," *Fortune* (February 21, 1994), p. 42.

20. W. Parker, "Visionary Leadership," *Selling Power* (April, 1998), p. 30.

Chapter 7

1. D. Liebeskind, "Reengineering R&D Work Processes," *Research Technology Management,* Vol. 41, No. 2, March/April 1998, p. 43.

2. B. Fitzgerald and C. Murphy, "Business Process Reengineering: Putting Theory into Practice," *Inform,* Vol. 34, No. 1, February 1996, p. 3.

3. J. Lawlor, "Mentoring Meets Networking in Formal Programs," *The Wall Street Journal* (November 30, 1997), p. 8.

4. C. Meyer, "How the Right Measures Help Teams Excel," *Harvard Business Review,* Vol. 72, No. 3, May/June 1994, p. 95.

5. D. Garvin, "Building a Learning Organization," *Harvard Business Review,* Vol. 71, No. 4, July/August 1993, p. 78.

6. A. Degeus, "Planning As Learning," *Harvard Business Review,* Vol. 66, No. 2, March/April 1988, p.70.

7. A. Ries and J. Trout, "Look Beyond the Hype for New Ideas," *Sales & Marketing Management Magazine* (June, 1994), p. 29.

8. J. Martin, "Strategy and the Art of Reinvesting Value," *Harvard Business Review,* Vol. 71, No. 5, September/October 1993, p. 39.

9. A. Kleiner and G. Roth, "How to Make Experience Your Company's Best Teacher" *Harvard Business Review,* Vol. 75, No. 5, September/October 1997, p. 172.

10. P. Druckor, E. Dyson, C. Handy, P. Saffo, and P. Senge, "Looking Ahead: Implications of the Present," *Harvard Business Review,* Vol. 75, No. 5, September/October 1997, p. 18.

11. P. Evans and T. Wurster, "Strategy and the New Economics of Information," *Harvard Business Review,* Vol. 75, No. 5, September/October 1997, p. 71.

12. G. Hamel, "Strategy As Revolution," *Harvard Business Review,* Vol. 74, No. 4, July/August 1996, p. 69.

13. J. Whitney, "Strategic Renewal for Business Units," *Harvard Business Review,* Vol. 74, No. 4, July/August 1996, p. 84.

14. P. Bromiley, R. Brown, and G. Shaw, "Strategic Stories: How 3 M Is Rewriting Business Planning," *Harvard Business Review,* Vol. 76, No. 3, May/June 1998, p. 41.

15. C. Christensen, "Making Strategy: Learning by Doing," *Harvard Business Review,* Vol. 75, No. 5, November/December 1997, p. 141.

16. B. O'Reilly, "How Execs Learn Now," *Fortune* (April 5, 1993), p. 52.

17. R. Henkoff, "Winning the New Career Game," *Fortune* (July 12, 1993), p. 46.

18. D. Cornachio, "How Not to Lose Your Job," *Sales & Marketing Management Magazine* (August, 1996), p. 58.

19. J. Fierman, "The Contingency Work Force," *Fortune* (January 24, 1994), p. 30.

20. S. Garland, K. Pennar, and E. Roberts, "Economic Anxiety," *Business Week* (March 11, 1996), p. 50.

21. R. Henkoff, "Companies That Train Best," *Fortune* (March 22, 1993), p. 62.

Chapter 8

1. M. Dawson, "Reengineer This!" *Systems Management,* Vol. 23, No. 4, April 1995, p. 44.

2. A. Barua and A. Winston, "Getting the Most out of Reengineering," *Booz-Allen Consulting Quarterly,* No. 7, 1998, p. 13.

3. S. Goldman, R. Nagel, and K. Preiss, *Agile Competitors and Virtual Organizations,* New York: Van Nostrand Reinhold, 1995.

4. D. Kirkpatrick, "Could AT&T Rule the World?" *Fortune* (May 17, 1993), p. 55.

5. K. Labich, "Was Breaking up AT&T a Good Idea?" *Fortune* (January 2, 1989), p. 82.

6. T. Carter, "Sales and Marketing Management and Reengineering," *International Association of Management Proceedings, Montreal, Canada,* Vol. 15, No. 1, 1997, pp. 139-145.

7. J. Mallgrave, "Business Reengineering for Survival," *Credit Union Executive,* Vol. 38, No. 2, March/April 1998, p. 4.

8. T. Carter, *Contemporary Sales Force Management,* Binghamton, NY: The Haworth Press, Inc., 1998.

9. W. Kiechel, "How We Will Work in the Year 2000," *Fortune* (May 17, 1993), p. 38.

10. N. Augustine, "Reshaping an Industry: Lockhead Martin's Survival Story," *Harvard Business Review,* Vol. 75, No. 3, May/June 1997, p. 83.

11. S. Haeckel and Richard Nolan, "Managing by Wire," *Harvard Business Review,* Vol. 71, No. 5, September/October 1993, p. 83.

12. R. Ashkenas, L. DeMonaco, and S. Francis, "Making the Deal Real: How GE Capital Integrates Acquisition," *Harvard Business Review,* Vol. 76, No. 1, January/February 1998, p. 165.

13. J. Main, "How to Steal the Best Ideas Around," *Fortune* (October 19, 1992), p. 102.

14. J. Graham, "The Business of Value," *Selling Power* (June 1996), p. 68.

15. J. Graham, "Turn Added Value into Added Sales," *Selling Power* (January/February 1995), p. 62.

Index

Page numbers followed by the letter "f" indicate figures; those followed by the letter "t" indicate tables.

Acute care facility, 141
Aftershock: Helping People Through Corporate Change, 51
Age of Job Stress, 24
Agile competition, 89
Airbus, layoffs at, 8
Alexander Group, Incorporated (The), 28
American Airlines, frequent flier program, 64
American Home Products Corporation, 14
American Institute of Stress, 23
American Management Association (AMA), 24, 25
American Quality Foundation, 145
Analysis/assessment/selection, 96
Andersen, Arthur, 81
Anger, 26
Apple, 121-122
Association of Executive Search Consultants, 28
AT&T, 133-134
Atwater Jr., H. Brewster, 11
Autonomy, employee, 52, 75-76

Balanced scorecard, 70-74
Bank One, 76
Bankers Trust, layoffs at, 7-8
Banking, 76-77
Barker, Jill, 33
Baselining, 98

Benchmarking, 124-125, 124f
Bentex Corporation, case study, 147-148
Black & Decker, and dynamic growth, 17
Boards, use of, 88-89
Boston University's Manufacturing Roundtable, 115
Builder mentality, 56t
Bureau of Labor Statistics, 27
Burke, James, 86-87
Burnout, job, 22-24
Business communication, 99-101, 102t importance of, 101
Business meeting, 103-104
Business process reengineering (BPR), 12, 67
Business research, 103-104
Businesspeople, smart, 57
"Buy in" to process, 37

California Management Review, 115
Case studies
    Bentex Corporation, 147-148
    Com Company, 18-19
    Dublin Incorporated, 32-33
    Monarch Wealth Management (MWM), 111-113
    Moore University Hospital, 52-53
    Okan Group, 89-91
    Reinglass Bank, 65-66
    Serxner Bank, 127-130
Categorical thinking, 51-52

Caution, 78
Change, resources for, 37
Change Management Team (CMT),
    16-17
Chase, 76
    layoffs at, 4
Cheating, to achieve work goals,
    25-26
Chief financial officers (CFOs), 68
China, reengineering in, 18
Chrysler, layoffs at, 7
Cigna, 133
Clean slate approach, 100
Cliques, and teamwork, 107
Colletti, Jerome, 28
Columbia. *See* Executive
    management education
Com Company (case study), 18-19
Commonwealth Fund, 30
Communication, 63-64. *See also*
    Business communication;
    Organizational communication
    effective, 101-102
    electronic, 123
Company practices, unfair, 23
Compensation, 26
Competition, 15, 60
Competitive advantage, 43
Competitive success, 116-119
Computers, 79. *See also* Technology
Conducting, business meeting, 103
Conference Board survey, 30
Conflict, 84
    teams and, 107
Core process. *See* Reengineering
Cost, evaluate, 78
Credit Watch, 5
Crisis management, 83-88, 84f
Culture change, 96, 98-99
Customer, 12, 56-65
    and builder mentality, 56f
    communicating with, 102
Customer focus, 63-64
Customer opportunity, IBM, 137-138

Customer perspective, 70. *See also*
    Balanced scorecard
Customer Relationship Assessment,
    Xerox, 62
Customer satisfaction, 60, 62-63
Cynicism, 26

Data General, layoffs at, 8
"Death by overwork," *karoshi*, 25
Decision-making mode, 14
"De-layering," 14
Delegation, task, 43, 47f
Dell, and IBM, 6
Demographics, 122
Deployment, 98
Depth, 100
Deregulation, 58
Design, of business processes, 98
Deterrence-based trust, 75
Development, 96, 99
Digital Equipment, layoffs at, 6-7
Dinsell, Craig, 89-91
Disillusion, and promotion, 14
Doing more with less, 38, 38f. *See
    also* Urgency theory
Dow Chemical, and customer
    satisfaction, 60
Downsizing, 30-31, 77. *See also*
    Reengineering
    and middle managers, 3
Dublin Incorporated, case study, 32-33
Dynamic growth, 17-18

Eastman Chemical, and customer
    satisfaction, 60
Eastman Kodak, 59
    layoffs at, 4-5
Economist, 145
Efficient organizations, 14-15
Electronic communication, 123
Electronic Data Systems (EDS), 59
E-mail, 81

:

Emotions, hair-trigger display of, 26
Employees
    burnout, job, 22-24
    and empowerment, 104-106
    and flex time, 31-32
    older, 30
    part-time, 126-127
    promotions, 14
    stress, 15, 22-24, 41, 44
    suicide, 15
    and teamwork. *See* Teamwork
    and uncertain future, 27
    violence, 15
    workload, increased, 23, 24-26
Employee ownership, 117-118
Employee performance, 51-52
Employment security, 116-117
Empowerment, 104-106
Enterprise level, and reengineering, 68
Ernst & Young, 145
Executive management education,
    125-126
Executive Recruiter, 126
External customer focus, 60
Extranet, 123

Families and Work Institute, 1993
    survey, 23
Fatigue, 26
Financial perspective, 70. *See also*
    Balanced scorecard
Flatter structure, 14
Flex time, 31-32, 45
Flexibility
    management, 39-40
    and outsourcing, 78
Follow-up, 63, 103
Forum Corporation, 63, 106
Forward-thinking organization,
    145-146
Foster Higgins & Company, 106
Frequent flier program, American
    Airlines, 64
Future, uncertain for worker, 27

General Mills, layoffs at, 11
Gerstner, Louis, 62, 63
Global competition, 40
Globalization, 32
Growth managers, 18
GTE, layoffs at, 11
Guilt, parental, 27

Harris, Louis, 106
Harrison, Lee Hecht, 30
Harvard. *See* Executive management
    education
Hay Group, 27, 106
Health care, and reengineering,
    140-143, 140f
Hewlett-Packard (HP), 138-140
High wages, 117
Hiring, industry experts, 57
HP Video server, 139. *See also*
    Hewlett-Packard (HP)
Huls America, 40
Human side, of reengineering, 12

IBM ("Big Blue")
    and customer satisfaction, 60, 62
    layoffs at, 5-6, 15
    restructuring sales force, 135-138
Identity, 84
Imbalanced alignment, 60
Improved efficiency, 44-45
Identification-based trust, 75
Individualized benefits, 58
Industry expert, hiring, 57
Industry Week, 27
Innovation, 98
Innovation perspective, 70. *See also*
    Balanced scorecard
Insufficient process breadth, 95
Integration, 72-73
Integration management, 145-146
Internal commitment, 105
Internal perspective, 70. *See also*
    Balanced scorecard

Internet, 80, 79f, 123
  banks, 77
Intranet, 123

Job description, 144
Job reduction. *See* Layoffs
Job skills, 144
Johnson & Johnson, and crisis
      management, 86-87
J.P. Morgan, layoffs at, 6

Karoshi, "death by overwork," 25
Kilts, James M., 9
KLM, layoffs at, 8
Knowledge-based trust, 75
Korn/Ferry International, 88

Layoffs, 4-11, 31. *See also individual
      companies*
Leadership, 29, 110-111
Learning, 85
Learning organization, 123-126, 124f
Leveraged buyouts (LBOs), 24
Levi Strauss & Company, layoffs at,
      49-51
Little, Arthur D., 21
Loyalty, to employer, 27

Management information systems
      (MIS), 66
Management skill base, 28-30
Management tools
  balanced scorecard, 70-74
  boards, 88-89
  business process reengineering
      (BPR), 67-68
  business reengineering, 68-69
  council, 88-89
  crisis management, 83-88
  modularity, 82-83
  outsourcing, 77-78

Management tools (*continued*)
  process redesign, 67-68
  risk management, 83-88
  technology, 78-82, 79f
  virtual offices, 74-77
Managers. *See also* Management
      tools; Middle managers
  Change Management Team
      (CMT), 16-17
  and cheating, 25-26
  and communication, 102
  and customers, 57, 63-64, 65
  and delegation, task, 43, 47f
  education, 125-126
  growth, 18
  and leadership, 29
  and reengineering, 13f, 14, 29f,
      69f
  and time efficiency, 46
Market focus, 55
Marsiello, Laura, 65, 66
Measurement, and management
      process, 120-123
Measurement system, performance,
      119-120
Meeting, business, 103-104
Mentors, 116
Middle managers, 29, 29t. *See also*
      Management tools; Manager
  and cheating, 25
  and communication, 99-100
  and crisis management, 86-88
  and downsizing, 3
  empowering lower-level
      employees, 39-40
  and flexibility, 39-40
  and long work hours, 25
  and loyalty, 27
  and urgency theory, 37
Mobile workforce, IBM, 137
Modularity, 82-83
Monarch Wealth Management
      (MWM), case study, 111-113
Monitoring in outsourcing process,
      78

Moore University Hospital, case study, 52-53
Motorola
layoffs at, 9
and outsourcing, 79
Multimedia presentations, 81-82

Nabisco, layoffs at, 9-10
Networking, 126
Networks, 64-65
Newton Message Pad, 121
Notebook PC, IBM, 137
Nursing, 141-142

Objectives, setting, 78
Okan Group, case study, 89-91
Older workers, 30
Opinion Research Corporation, 105-106
Organization, 67-68
Organizational communication, 95, 102t
Organizational learning, 123-126, 124f
"Out of sight, out of mind," 121
"Outside the box," 12
Outsourcing, 77-78
Outstanding corporate strategy, 121

Palmer, Robert B., 7
Participation, and empowerment, 105-106
Partnering, 63
Part-time employment, 126-127
Pay-for-skills system, 109
Peers, communicating with, 102
Pennsylvania State Employees credit Union, 143
Pepsi-Cola, and crisis management, 87-88
Performance, employee, 51-52
Performance appraisal, 26

Performance measurement systems, 119-120
Performance review, 88-89
Personal Lending Group, 128
Personal restructuring, 143-145
Pitney Bowes Management Service, 104
Planning, 98, 103, 123
Point-of-sale (POS), 136
Power, 84, 109
Priority Management survey, 23, 24
Process, 55-56, 59, 67-68
definition of, 95
Process innovation. *See* Reengineering
Process redesign, 67
Profitable growth, 18
Promotions
from within, 119
and reengineering, 14

Questionnaire, director, 89
Qwest Communication International, 11

Radical improvement, 96. *See also* Reengineering
Radical redesign, 98. *See also* Reengineering
Ralston Purina, and customer satisfaction, 60
Reengineering, 4t, 12-14, 13t. *See also individual companies*
business, 68-69
case studies. *See* Case studies
in China, 18
consequences, 21-22, 22t
and crisis management, 83-88, 84f
and customers, 56-65
and builder mentality, 56f
definition of, *xi*
effective, 39-40, 68-69, 69f, 147
achieving, 97f
goals of, 96-99, 97f

Reengineering (*continued*)
  and health care, 140-143, 140f
  human side of, 22-27, 96
  need, determining, 61f
  and process, 55-56, 59
Regional sales managers (RSMs),
    128-130
Reinglass Bank, case study, 65-66
ReliaStar Insurance Company, 1992
    survey, 23
Research, business, 103-104
Retention program, 64
Rhythm, managing, 45. *See also*
    Time pacing
"Right-sizing," 14, 30. *See also*
    Reengineering
Risk management, 83-88
Roberts, Jason, 18-19

Sales/marketing professional, 44-45
Sanger, Mark, 11
Schumpeter, Joseph, 18
Securities Data Company, 145
Self-criticism, 26
Serxner Bank, case study, 127-130
Siemens, Atlanta, 64
Skill development, 118
Sociability, 107
Sprung, Calvin, 52-53
St. Paul Fire & Marine, 1992 survey,
    23
Stages, business research, 104
Standard & Poor's Rating Agency, 5
Strategic fundamentals, 122
Strategy, 72, 123. *See also* Balanced
    scorecard
Stress, employee, 15, 22-24, 41, 44
Structural team, 108f
Subordinates, communicating with,
    102
Substance abuse, and job stress, 23, 24
Suicide, job-related, 15
Sunbeam, layoffs at, 10
Supervision, poor, 23

Taco Bell, 122
Targeting, 96, 98
Team selling, 139-140
Teamwork, 106-111, 108f
  lack of, 23
  Levi Strauss & Company, 49-51
  and trust, 74-75
Technology, 67-68, 78-82, 79f
Temp. *See* Part-time employment
360-degree feedback, 107
3M, and customer satisfaction, 60
Time conservation, 47f
Time efficiency, 45-46, 46f-48f, 49
Time pacing, 45-46, 46f-48f, 49
Time pressure, 49
Total Quality Management (TQM),
    16
Towers Perrin, 106
Training, 96, 99, 118
Transformation, 98
Transition, managing, 45. *See also*
    Time pacing
Trust, and teamwork, 74-75
Turnover, and job burnout, 23
Two-way information flow, 58, 100
"Tylenol decision," 86-87

Underpopulation, 122
Undervalued, employees feeling, 52
Unified sales strategy (USS), 111
Universal Card, 134
Upward evaluation, 106-107
Urgency theory, 40-51, 42t

Value, 71, 121
Value focus, 58-59
Value-added features, 59-60, 61f
Verbal communication, 101
Videoconferencing, 81
Violence, employee, 15
Virtual offices, 74-77
Vision, 72. *See also* Balanced
    scorecard
Volatile business environment, 28t

Wages, high, 117
Workers, and reengineering. *See*
    Employee
Workload
  cutting back on, 27
  increased, 24-26
    and burnout, 22-24
  unreasonable, 23
World Wide Web, 77, 80-81
Written communication, 101

Xerox
  Customer Relationship
    Assessment, 62
  and customer satisfaction, 60, 62
  layoffs at, 10

Yankelovich Monitor, and job stress,
  22

Order Your Own Copy of
This Important Book for Your Personal Library!

THE AFTERMATH OF REENGINEERING
Downsizing and Corporate Performance

_____ in hardbound at $34.95 (ISBN: 0-7890-0720-7)

COST OF BOOKS _____

OUTSIDE USA/CANADA/
MEXICO: ADD 20% _____

POSTAGE & HANDLING _____
(US: $3.00 for first book & $1.25
for each additional book)
Outside US: $4.75 for first book
& $1.75 for each additional book)

SUBTOTAL _____

IN CANADA: ADD 7% GST _____

STATE TAX _____
(NY, OH & MN residents, please
add appropriate local sales tax)

FINAL TOTAL _____
(If paying in Canadian funds,
convert using the current
exchange rate. UNESCO
coupons welcome.)

☐ **BILL ME LATER:** ($5 service charge will be added)
(Bill-me option is good on US/Canada/Mexico orders only;
not good to jobbers, wholesalers, or subscription agencies.)

☐ Check here if billing address is different from
shipping address and attach purchase order and
billing address information.

Signature _____

☐ **PAYMENT ENCLOSED:** $ _____

☐ **PLEASE CHARGE TO MY CREDIT CARD.**

☐ Visa   ☐ MasterCard   ☐ AmEx   ☐ Discover
☐ Diner's Club

Account # _____

Exp. Date _____

Signature _____

Prices in US dollars and subject to change without notice.

NAME _____

INSTITUTION _____

ADDRESS _____

CITY _____

STATE/ZIP _____

COUNTRY _____ COUNTY (NY residents only) _____

TEL _____ FAX _____

E-MAIL_____
May we use your e-mail address for confirmations and other types of information? ☐ Yes   ☐ No

Order From Your Local Bookstore or Directly From
The Haworth Press, Inc.
10 Alice Street, Binghamton, New York 13904-1580 • USA
TELEPHONE: 1-800-HAWORTH (1-800-429-6784) / Outside US/Canada: (607) 722-5857
FAX: 1-800-895-0582 / Outside US/Canada: (607) 772-6362
E-mail: getinfo@haworthpressinc.com
PLEASE PHOTOCOPY THIS FORM FOR YOUR PERSONAL USE.

BOF96